HOW TO WIN THE CHAMPIONSHIP

Date: 1/30/12

**795.412 CLO
Cloutier, T. J.
How to win the
championship /**

ABOUT THE AUTHOR

T.J. Cloutier has won 59 major poker tournament titles, more than any other player in the world. His 20-years-plus career at the World Series of Poker includes 39 final table appearances, the world record.

Cloutier has placed in the top five of the championship event four times, starting in 1985 when he placed second to Bill Smith. He came in fifth place in 1988, the year that Johnny Chan beat Erik Seidel, a victory immortalized by Matt Damon in the movie Rounders. In 1998 T.J. placed third to Scotty Nguyen. His most notable final-table appearance came in 2000 when he was runner-up to Chris Ferguson. In fact the 2000 WSOP final-table play has become a classic among poker aficionados.

Winning the $5,000 no-limit event at the 2005 WSOP catapulted T.J.'s tournament winnings to $5,495,553, putting him in sixth place on the international money-won list, and increasing his bracelet count to six. "Just like fine wine, T.J. Cloutier gets better with age," WSOP Media Director Nolan Dalla wrote after T.J. won it.

"I'm not ready for the pasture just yet," T.J. responded. "I still have a few more wins left in me." And thankfully, at least one more book. "At the seminars I do, everybody asks me about how to play the final table, so I figured it was time to write a book on how to master the endplay in a tournament."

Many players credit *Championship No-Limit & Pot-Limit Hold'em*, T.J. Cloutier's first book with co-author Tom McEvoy, for helping them win megabucks at major tournaments. Joseph Hachen, 2005 World Champion of Poker, endorsed his teaching abilities: "T.J. Cloutier's book is the book that I learned the most from. It gives you a sound basis and understanding of the game." T.J.'s other books include *Championship Hold'em*, *Championship Hold'em Tournament Hands*, and *Championship Omaha*.

HOW TO WIN THE CHAMPIONSHIP

T.J. CLOUTIER

CARDOZA
PUBLISHING

Cardoza Publishing is the foremost gaming publisher in the world, with a library of over 175 up-to-date and easy-to-read books and strategies. These authoritative works are written by the top experts in their fields and with more than 8,500,000 books in print, represent the best-selling and most popular gaming books anywhere.

FIRST EDITION

Copyright © 2006 by T.J. Cloutier
- All Rights Reserved -

Library of Congress Catalog Card No: 2005920554
ISBN: 1-58042-166-0

Visit our web site—www.cardozapub.com—or write for a full list of books and computer strategies.

CARDOZA PUBLISHING
P.O. Box 1500, Cooper Station, New York, NY 10276
Phone (800) 577-WINS
email: cardozapub@aol.com
www.cardozapub.com

TABLE OF CONTENTS

Try to Increase Your Chips at Each Level
Recognize the Impact of the Antes and Blinds
Be Aware of Your Table Position in Relation to the Big Stacks
Take Note of Your Place on the Curve
Get to Know the Nature of Your Opponents
Always Make Quality Decisions

INTRODUCTION

by Dana Smith

A lot of people play no-limit hold'em well enough to make it through the opening rounds of big-field tournaments in good shape. But very few players know how to finish well—and even fewer know the secrets of getting to the final three spots and grabbing the brass ring.

Take the case of Paul Player, who has been playing tournament poker for three years. He has made the money a time or two in $100 events, and has come close to cracking some major money in the $500 and $1,000 tournaments he's experimented with. But he also seems to run into a brick wall when he gets to one table away from the money. That's when his nerves start to unravel and his game crumbles. If this scenario sounds biographical, *How to Win the Championship* is the book for you.

Legendary tournament champion T. J. Cloutier teaches you how to build up enough chips to make it from one table out of the money to the final table. You will learn the strategies that have taken him to the championship table of more tournaments than any other player in poker. T.J. explains the theory, the how-to, the why-to, and the when-to of money-table tournament play in the easy-to-understand language that he has become famous for in his other poker books.

Starting with an explanation of the basic principles of tournament play, Cloutier takes you on a table-by-table journey through the jungle of tournament endplay. Along the way, you will learn many of the concepts he teaches in poker "boot camps" across the nation. Once you've made it to the final table, T.J. guides you through every step you must take to climb to the top of the tournament money ladder. Starting with nine finalists at the championship table, he details time-proven strategies for playing against six, three, and two opponents. Then he gives you the key moves you must make in heads-ups poker to win the title, the trophy, and the money.

Cloutier concludes his instruction by letting you get inside his mind as he reprises the play at the championship table of the 2005 World Series of Poker $5,000 No-Limit Hold'em tournament. Through his play-by-play analysis, you will discover how he won his sixth WSOP gold bracelet—and how you can join him at the championship table.

PART 1:

What Separates the Great Players from the Good Players

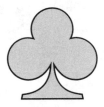

THE ATTRIBUTES OF GREAT PLAYERS

What separates great poker players from average players? I've been asked that question a zillion times over the years. Here are some of the characteristics that I believe distinguish perennial winners from one-time wonders.

1. GREAT PLAYERS MAKE VERY FEW MISTAKES

Poker is a game of mistakes. Nobody plays it perfectly but the best players make far fewer mistakes than anybody else. In final table play, any mistake you make could cost you a place, a lot of money. Earlier in the tournament, a major mistake may not knock you out. You can recover from it and still make it to the money. But at the final table, that same mistake is magnified because it can cost you a higher place in the tournament than you would have had if you hadn't made the mistake. It can even cost you the championship.

Not only do great players make very few mistakes, they know they're making a mistake *while* they're doing it, not *after* it's done. Before I make a play at the pot in a poker tournament, I ask myself "Should I do this now, or should I not?" Sometimes, I just say, "The hell with it, I'll just do it." And I pay for it! But I know I'm making a mistake while I'm doing it. Amateurs play hands they shouldn't play and they don't know they're making a mistake.

If you don't know you're making a mistake, how can you learn from it? Knowing when you've made a bad move is an instinct that develops from what you've learned over the years. When you see that a play doesn't work, chalk it up on your mental blackboard so that you can learn from it. Pay special attention to the hands you play out of position. New players make basic mistakes such as playing a 10-8 suited from up front, or playing a pair of deuces and then calling a raise with them.

Suppose you want to play an A-10 or some other marginal hand from up front. Your decision comes down to asking, "Should I play this hand up front now while we're playing 8-handed? I know that if I get raised and I call the raise, it will cost me a lot of my chips if I don't flop perfect to it." Or suppose the pot was raised and it comes with an ace. If you decide to play your weak ace on the flop and you're wrong, it becomes a glaring mistake that costs you a lot of money in a pot you shouldn't have played in the first place. My premise is that great players don't make those kinds of mistakes. And they don't do it year after year after year.

At one time in my life, I felt that I played flawless poker where I never made a mistake—the final table at the 2000 World Series of Poker. From the first hand dealt to the last hand dealt, I thought that I never made a mistake. That's the only time that I've ever claimed to play perfect poker. I've won a lot of tournaments, sure, but I've made mistakes in them. That one, I didn't.

Great players bring their A-game to the table with them. There's not a player alive who brings it with him every day, but top players play their A-game throughout the tournament a lot more often than average players. It's like any other sport or job—the guys who are really good at what they do get the cheese over time.

2. GREAT PLAYERS HAVE AN INNATE SENSE OF TIMING

I believe that in any poker game, the best players have a superior sense of timing that is rooted in what they've learned over the years. Timing is an offshoot of instinct and observation. If you've played a lot of poker, your instincts will tell you what to do. Your mind has learned all this stuff, and your subconscious will kick it back to you in particular situations. For example, you'll have pocket fives, somebody raises the pot, and you throw them away. And you do that time and again, throwing away small pocket pairs. "Muck 'em," your mind tells you. "You don't need to play this pot." Then all of a sudden, your subconscious says, "Call!" You follow your instinct, you call—and you win the pot with a hand you have correctly folded a zillion times in the past.

It's like ESP and it works. I've always had a pretty good sense of when I can make a play and who I can make it against. A sense of timing is akin to instinct. And instinct is something that you can't teach. Some players are just born with an innate sense of timing, and there are other players, like me, whose sense of timing comes from a combination of what I've learned over the years through observation, and the memory skills I was born with.

Knowing when to try to steal the blinds requires a sense of timing, but it's also an instinctive move. I like to pick up the blinds, but I prefer picking up raises. It's when you try to do it that counts. Say that Joe raises the pot and you've been watching him play for a long time. You know that he raises on marginal hands when he's sitting in certain positions, but he's a good enough player that he doesn't stand reraises with marginal hands. So, you reraise him. Now you've won not only the blinds and antes, you've won a raised pot, which will usually pay for three or four rounds of the deal when you're not holding hands. That's the way I've done it for years.

I've gone for three to four hours in a poker tournament when two fives or two sixes were the biggest hands I've held, and I probably didn't play them. But almost invariably, I've had more chips at the end of that round than I started with just by making situational plays based on timing and instinct. I would say that one out of ten times, I'll make a play at the pot and I'll be wrong. But one out of ten isn't a bad percentage.

Some readers have told me, "Well, T.J., you talk about instinct and timing, but you don't tell us how to get it." You get it by playing, by observing, paying attention to the game, learning the game. When I say learn the game, I mean you learn the *game*—not only what the cards tell you, but what the players tell you. And I don't mean what they tell you with their mouths—what they tell you by the way they play.

I played in a televised tournament with eight proven players that was broadcast on Super Bowl Sunday. And I learned something that I never knew before about three different players—because I paid attention from the first day. I made a study of their play throughout the five days we played to see if they did it the same way every time. And they did. I learned something important about three top players that you wouldn't think you could learn from players of that caliber, things about their play that I could use later on when we're playing together. You never stop learning.

The things that you learn become the foundation of your instincts. In Super System, Doyle Brunson labels it "recall." It's what I call "playing the game." You're not just playing your hand, you're playing the *game*. Even when you're not in the hand, you're playing the game because you're learning something by observing the players who are in the hand. Nobody is good enough that they can't learn, no matter who they are.

3. GREAT PLAYERS KNOW HOW TO MAKE MORE MONEY ON A HAND

Another thing that separates great players from average players is that a great player can play the same hand against the same hand, and the great player will make more money on it than an amateur will. An inexperienced player might have a hand, bet it on the flop, and bet it again on fourth street. Then he decides to show it down on fifth street, figuring that he's already made enough money on the hand. But the great player won't miss that last bet. He will bet it on fifth street, and get paid off there too. He's not worried about that certain card that came off on the river.

If you're willing to call a bet on the end, why not make a bet on the end? Always keep this in your mind. If you're a good enough player, you'll throw the hand away if you get raised and think you're beaten. But since you were going to call a regular bet anyway, why not bet it on the end. You see this happen in limit poker all the time, and quite often in no-limit games:

Bet, bet, show down. It becomes a pattern with some players. But the great player who goes ahead and bets the hand on the river, and gets paid off, will get more money out of the same hand than the amateur will. In other words, the better players will use the best betting strategy to get the most value out of their hands.

The example above involves the bet-bet-bet rather than the bet-bet-call. Of course it only holds true when you think you have the hand to bet with. Obviously, if you're bluffing and you bet-bet and get called both times, there's nothing wrong with shutting down if you haven't made something by fifth street. A lot of times when I start off bluffing, I go ahead and fire three barrels—but the minute I sense that I am beaten, I shut down.

On fifth street, the top players never make a call when they've put somebody on a hand that can beat them. An amateur might be thinking "Well, if he has such and such, I can beat that hand, so I'm gonna call." Instead he should be thinking "He has such and such, and I can't beat that hand, so I'm folding." There might be five possible hands on board that the amateur can't beat, and one possible hand he can beat—and he puts his opponent on the one hand he can beat to justify making the call.

For example, suppose there's a K-Q-10-5-3 on the board, and you have pocket nines. There's every possibility that you will lose this hand, but you can beat two eights and two sevens, or ace-baby, right?

So you call. You've put him on a hand that you can beat, not one of the many hands you can't beat. Sure enough, your opponent has two pair or a straight and you wind up burning up your chips. Experts never do that.

What gets my hackles up when I'm playing a tournament is someone who says, "How could that guy have made that play against me?" as he leaves the table broke. And I think to myself, "If everybody played the same way, poker would be a hand-holding contest." You'd better hope that people are making those kinds of plays.

Another way that good players make more money on their hands is the way in which they handle three checks. It's very hard for some players to stand three checks to them after the flop. After that third check on the river, they just have to bet. And if their opponent is laying a trap and check-raises them on the river, they wind up losing chips they didn't need to lose. You don't need to feel pressured into betting in this situation.

A very good player can handle three checks. Using his sense of timing, the good player can check behind his opponent. Or if he senses that his opponent doesn't have anything, he will make a bet and take the pot. He may not have a hand himself, but he bets because his instincts tell him that his opponent doesn't have anything either. When he was playing a lot of limit hold'em tournaments, Mike Laing was a master at this play. When he was in a pot, there were no showdowns. He won every pot that ordinarily would have been shown down at the end, whether or not he had a hand. Mike has a great sense for knowing when his opponents don't have a hand. He often makes this play in no-limit tournaments too, and he gets a hold of a lot of chips that way.

4. EXPERTS DON'T BURN UP THEIR CHIPS

Great players know that every bad call they *don't* make is the same as a win. This is a basic truth in poker. A great player knows that if he doesn't make a call here and a call there, the money he has left after saving those calls is the same as winning a pot. It makes the difference in the money he has available to raise a pot later on in the game. All those "long" calls that players make on the end, especially in limit poker when they say they're calling because of the size of the pot, probably will make the difference in the amount they've won or lost for the day.

A lot of times you'll see a player make long calls from the flop on. The flop might come J-10-4 and he has an A-4. An opponent makes a small bet and the A-4 calls it. On fourth street comes a 5 or 6, a nothing card. His opponent makes another small bet and the A-4 says to himself "I'm gonna call one more time. I might spike an ace or a four on the river," not thinking that maybe the bettor has a K-Q and if an ace comes on fifth street, the A-4 will lose the hand. Then the flop blanks off on the end, and he's lost two bets because he can't legitimately call with bottom pair. He's just burned up his chips. But great players don't burn up their chips. They have the chips in front of them so that they can play when they finally get a hand.

The bet-call, bet-call, bet-call is a type of play more likely to be made by a player coming out of the limit hold'em ranks into the no-limit ranks. However a lot of people are starting off in poker by playing no-limit hold'em. They're beginning by playing online and they see a lot of draw-outs in the little online tournaments. Instead of learning the things they should be picking up from the game, they start thinking "Hey, look at the pot that guy won because he made the call on the end." They don't realize how seldom that happens. All they see is that he won a big pot by calling. Then when they play a big tournament in a casino, they do the same thing. The result? They burn up their chips looking for that miracle card and end up looking for the lobby.

5. TRUE CHAMPIONS HAVE STOOD THE TEST OF TIME

Great players have a track record against top competition over a long length of time. I'm not talking about the little daily tournaments, I'm talking about big-league tournaments with buy-ins of $1,000 or more. In the old days, it used to be $500 or more, but now that tournaments have escalated, the big tournaments start at $1,000 buy-ins.

I see a lot of poker wonders come along who do well for one or two years, and then you never hear of them again. It's happened time and time again. But great players have stood the test of time—players like Doyle Brunson, Chip Reese, Howard Lederer, Phil Hellmuth, Erik Seidel, Tom McEvoy, and Johnny Chan—and have been winning big tournaments for years and years and years. At the end of the year, they get the money. If they played the same crew all year long, they would end up winners. And the reason they get the money is because they play the game the way it should be played.

The great players have paid their dues. You put in your dues learning how to play. When they first started out, a lot of successful players got broke playing poker. In the old days when I first started playing, I got broke a lot of times. But you get up the next day and say, "This is a new day, let's go get 'em."

When everyone sits down at the table, the great player is the one that everybody else notices first. "Oh, no! You're at my table?" they say. I hear it all the time. A less experienced player thinks, "Well, I know I can't win now, but at least I can get some experience, and then I can go home and tell folks that I played against so-and-so." Whether they mean it or not, it's still a form of respect. Great players are the players that everybody knows, respects, and fears.

You also pay your dues by starting small and then building up to higher games and tournaments. You won't find somebody coming in new and winning a big tournament with no experience whatsoever at playing little tournaments. A lot of today's best tournament players took up tournament play after playing high limits in live games, but they worked up to the high games by first playing in small games. Even Doyle and Chip started off playing much smaller stakes than they play these days. Of course there were games in those days when a thousand or two thousand dollars was a big win, even in no-limit hold'em.

There is a core of great players who have been playing winning poker for years, and there also are several young players on the rise—Allen Cunningham, Daniel Negreanu, John Juanda, Phil Ivey and Layne Flack. Poker has some very good female players too: Annie Duke, Jennifer Harmon, Cindy Violette, Nani Dollison, Marsha Waggoner, Barbara Enright, Kathy Leibert, and Maureen Feduniak.

PART 2

The Basic Principles of Play for Getting to the Championship Table

A lot of people can play tournaments well, but very few know how to finish well. Take the case of John Doe, who has been playing tournament poker for three years. He's almost made the big money a time or two, but hasn't yet succeeded in taking any of it home with him. When the action gets down to 30-40 players in a tournament that pays 27 places, his game crumbles. Sound familiar?

In this section you will learn how several important factors influence optimal tournament strategy when you're close to the money table in tournaments.

A lot of players would swim across Lake Tahoe if they could just get into the money in a major tournament. That would be their lifetime accomplishment. Just making it to the money involves one set of goals but winning the tournament requires a different set. I have one goal every time I sit down in a tournament: To win it. I never, I mean *never*, think of just getting into the money. I believe that when you set your goal to win the tournament, you have a mind set that's a lot different from just trying to get into the money. And you treat situations differently.

SET YOUR GOAL FOR THE TOURNAMENT

What is your goal? Ask yourself, "Am I satisfied with getting into the money, or am I trying to win the tournament?" Obviously, you have to have chips to win, but the way you go about getting them might differ according to your goals. If you get dealt two jacks, do you play conservatively and just call with them, hoping to flop a jack? Or do you raise with them and take the chance of losing some chips if you get called?

When your goal is just getting into the money, you consider things such as stack size, antes and blinds, and table position. Then you ask yourself "How do I stack up with everybody else at the other tables?" All you're trying to do is survive. You're running around from table to table seeing how everybody else is doing. You don't have to do that. I never get up from my table to find out what all the stack sizes are because I know what it takes to get to the money: I know that as players go out, I have to start increasing my chips.

If you're just trying to get to the money, you tend to forget a lot of no-limit hold'em betting strategies that you can use to get the chips. You might hesitate, wondering "If I play very conservatively, can I get to the money?" when you should be asking, "If I take a few chances here and there, will I have a better chance to win the tournament?" Or, "Are the cards running over me today so that I can still go deep into the tournament without having to take many chances?" You have to figure out what you're trying to accomplish with your tournament strategy and factor in how things are going for you that day.

In my strategy, the first time that I really start thinking about getting a hold of chips is when we get to one table away from the money-36 players if they're paying 27 places, for example. Up to that point, I want to outlast everybody and give myself a chance to win the tournament. Remember that you can't win a tournament during the first few hours, but you sure as hell can lose it! So you play pretty conservatively early in the tournament. When you get down to one table from the money—with winning the tournament as your goal—that is when you really start playing to win. It isn't that I start playing more hands, but I definitely go in search of getting chips at that level.

Aggressive is a good word for my approach. I open up my game and play a little more, take a few more chances and play my opponent a little stronger in certain situations. I find out which players I think are just trying to get to the money, and I try to take advantage of that situation.

If you watch carefully, you can tell that Player A is ecstatic to get this far in the tournament. He doesn't think he can win it, but he'd sure like to get to the money. Attack him! He's a good prospect to steal some money from, the type of opponent you can win some pots from. He'll make that first call, but he might not make that second call because he's saying to himself "Boy, that'll cost me a lot of money," giving you the advantage to take his chips. For sure he won't make that second call if he's on a draw, or if he has second or third pair.

You might be sitting there with nothing much, but knowing what you know about Player A, you can open up your game a little bit against him. If you do it in a way that isn't too reckless, you can win some chips in those situations. I'm not talking about moving all in, but simply betting an amount that will win the pot for you.

BE CAREFUL BEFORE YOU DECIDE TO MOVE ALL IN

Too many people think that playing no-limit hold'em tournaments equates to moving all your chips in a lot of the time. That "All in!" move that you see so often on television is not the only play you can make in no-limit hold'em. The correct play is to do whatever the situation calls for—that's how you determine the size of your bets.

You do not have to sacrifice all your chips when you're making a play at a pot. Just risk a decent amount, so that you're still in the ballgame if your play doesn't work. You don't have to send a man to do a boy's job. So why not bet like a boy? Instead of betting $5,000, bet $1,000. A lot of times, betting one grand will get the same job done as betting five grand, and with far less risk. If you have a great hand, and you know that your opponent will pay you off if you move in, obviously you move in. But if you think he'll only pay off $500, you only bet $500. The idea is to bet the proper amount in the proper situation at the right time.

Now, when you know that you have the best hand and you want to protect it—and you're just trying to get to the money—you might make a big bet, hoping that your opponents will throw their hands away. And you'll just win what's in the pot, instead of playing it like most great players. Expert players want to play the pot out because they know they can play better than you can as the streets go along, and they'll win more money on the pot than you would. Great players always try to get the maximum value from their good hands.

You're going to hold some hands, and you're going to win some pots. It's the little pots you win when you aren't holding a hand that probably will make the difference in the long run. You just have to be careful about who you try to make moves against. As I said, I try to do it against the players who I know would be happy as hell just to make it to the money. If I want to pick up a pot, I pick it up from them, not from the guy who's going gung-ho.

The other thing you need to recognize before you try making a move is who's holding cards at your table. Everybody's going to hold cards at some point, but who's holding cards right now? Invariably there's somebody who's going to hold four or five hands in a row. You don't want to play somebody's rush for him. Luck is streaky, so I make it a point to stay out of a guy's way if I see that he's streaking, or raising two or three pots in a row. Certainly you don't want to play any marginal hands against him.

One day in a tournament, I had raised two pots in

a row and was about to come into the big blind on the next hand. The first time I had pocket tens; the second time I had A-K. "You know, if somebody raises three pots in a row," I said to the players at the table, "and aces weren't the first hand he held, the third raise in a row is usually his biggest hand." As soon as the words had come out of my mouth, I looked down and there they were—two aces in the big blind, the first time I'd had them all day long. A couple of players limped in, I raised, and boy they folded fast! "See what I mean?" I told them, and I turned over my pocket aces. That made believers out of them in a hurry.

TRY TO INCREASE YOUR CHIPS AT EACH LEVEL

If you can get to every break in the tournament with more money than you had at the last break, you're doing well. You want to keep increasing your stack size at every level, but you don't have to double up; you just want to have more chips.

The time when you have to get a hold of the chips is just before you go to the final table, or at the final table. That's when you want to open up your play a little bit. You want to get enough chips so that when you hit the final table, you're comfortable. Very few players are capable of taking a very small stack and going through the whole table to win the tournament. It happens, but invariably it's like a horse race when a horse breaks bad out of the gate. He catches up to the field and he gets the lead, but he's used everything he has just to get to the field. And he dies in the stretch. It's the same thing in poker. You'll beat this guy, you'll beat that guy, and then you'll beat another guy, and you start building up your chips. But then suddenly, you'll hit a stone wall. You get a good hand and you make a play—and you're gone.

I was invited to play in a special tournament for television in which eight of the best players in the world were playing against each other. Doyle Brunson had the small stack when we started, and he built it up to where he was in second position in the chip count. He finally picked up two queens—and he ran into two aces! The flop came something like five or six high, and they got it all in on the flop. I mean he was gone in a New York minute. This is what I'm talking about. A lot of times that small stack just can't quite get there at the end. And I'm using one of the best players who ever lived as proof of the pudding.

If you have a lot of chips, I'm not saying to just sit back on them and simply skate to the final table. But don't do too much playing around either. Suppose three tables are left, and you have the most chips. Just continue doing what you've been doing rather than opening up. Play solid poker and stay away from draws. You would be very happy to go to the final table with the amount of chips you already have.

RECOGNIZE THE IMPACT OF THE ANTES AND BLINDS

The amount of the antes and blinds in relation to the size of your stack definitely affect your play. Say that it's down to three tables and the blinds are $800-$1600 with a $200 ante. It's costing you $4,200 just to play a round. If you're short-stacked, you just have to find two cards you like and get in there with them. When I say "two cards you like," they don't necessarily need to be A-K. You might be dealt Q-J, J-10 or J-9—marginal hands that you usually can't stand raises with—and now you're raising with them. You're trying to get your little bit of chips in action. You might be up against a lesser hand and win the pot with a raise. Just be sure to do something before you get so low on chips that no matter what you do, it won't help you.

Say that you have $5,000 in chips and you're playing $800-$1600 blinds. I would want to make my move in that area. Then if I make a play at a pot, I'm picking up around $4,200 (the money that's already in the pot), so I'm going to almost double my stack if I win the pot even if nobody calls me. And that's very nice. You know that if you're playing nine-handed, you're going to be back in the very same situation if you don't play another hand by the time the blinds come back to you.

When you're short stacked, the frequency of the

hands you play has to pick up a little bit so that you can start building your stack. Or you have to get two or three-way action in a pot, and win it. Hopefully, you're going to have a hand, but you also don't want to ante yourself down to the point where it doesn't matter.

For example, if you're down to $2,500 and you win $2,500, you're still right back to the $5,000 level. You haven't accomplished anything. It's still going to cost you $4,200 a round so you still have basically only eight or nine hands to choose from before you have to post the blinds again. And you don't want to get back to $2,500 again because if you win, you'll be right back in the same situation again.

BE AWARE OF YOUR TABLE POSITION IN RELATION TO THE BIG STACKS

Your table position in respect to where the big stacks are sitting at your table is important. If you're the big stack, that's great—your position is *the* position at the table. If you have the most chips, it doesn't matter who's on your left or who's on your right. Your chip position compensates for your seat position, for everything.

But if you're a medium stack and a big stack is sitting to your left, or if there are two big stacks at the table and they're both to your left, you're in a bad situation a lot of times. However I wouldn't let that change my criteria for how I play. If you have a medium stack, you have enough chips to play with, so play a hand, and hope that those two big stacks play with you because they can double you up. Just keep in mind that any time you get all your chips in against a big stack, they have you covered and you can go out of the tournament if you lose the hand. Obviously that can't happen if you're all in against a smaller stack.

It doesn't matter to me whether I'm all in against a big stack or a short stack. But I'm going to try to have the right kind of hand in that spot to begin with, and hope that it holds up. I can advise you as to what to do in these situations, but your hand still has to hold up. And it seems like time after time, the worst hand goes against the odds and wins, though it obviously doesn't win any more often over a long period of time than it's supposed to. But in tournaments, those odds kick in a little late sometimes. People sometimes forget that in tournament play, you're not talking about long-term results—you're talking about getting lucky in the short term.

TAKE NOTE OF YOUR PLACE ON THE CURVE

When you're one table away from the money, you redraw for seating assignments. When that situation arises, there's nothing wrong with walking around to see how you stand against everybody else. When you're not playing a hand is the best time to do it. You can see how your chip position compares with the other players. This is the only time that I would ever get out of my seat to see where I stood. When you get back to playing, all you care about is your chip position at *your* table because that's the only place you have any control.

Now, I understand that when you're close to the money and you're kind of short stacked—there are a couple of other short stacks and you're one away from the money—that you might be worried. A lot of players worry in this situation because they want to get something back for their play. So, they won't play any hand, or they'll stall on a hand hoping that somebody else goes out, or they'll stall to buy some time before they have to post the blinds. This happens in every single tournament, and there's not much you can do about that.

A player in the $25,000 main event at the WPT championship one year almost got barred from the play. He was very low-stacked when we were on the bubble and playing hand for hand. Some other players also had very low stacks, and when the action got to him, he would just sit there forever before he would act on his hand. That was very poor form, ridiculous to say the least. They put the clock on him every hand. And guess what? He finally got something like two queens, got busted with them, and went out on the bubble. Just what he deserved, I thought.

When you're in the money, sure you want to gather chips, but don't rush. Don't make bad plays to try to get them. Suppose you have just an average number of chips. It's easy to figure the average. Just take the number of players still in action and divide that number into the amount of chips in play to tell how you stand in comparison to the rest of the field. If you just have average chips, you're right on par for the blinds; that is, you have enough chips to handle the size of the blinds. If you have one-half the average, you're in slight trouble. If you have only one-quarter the average, you're in big trouble, and you have to do something about it.

What if the average is $500,000 and you have $450,000? I wouldn't worry about it too much. I've heard players say, "I'm not even up to par. I've gotta play!" Baloney! They're making excuses. A lot of people make excuses to lose; that is, to find a way that makes them lose. Believe me, there are plenty of ways to lose. You don't have to use an excuse to find a way to lose! There are two zillion cards out there. And those cards and Lady Luck can be very, very fickle.

GET TO KNOW THE NATURE OF YOUR OPPONENTS

Always think about who is at your table, and how they're playing. By the time you get down to one table away from the money, you should be able to figure out who is doing what in which situations. If this guy has a big reputation, and that guy has a big reputation, usually it is well deserved. They can play. So, you have to change your play around a little bit, you can't be doing exactly the same thing every time. Say that you're running good and you pick up aces under the gun. If you decide to limp in with them one time, that's fine, but don't limp in with them the next time you get them. You want to change your play around so that they can't get a fix on you.

Make sure you have a read on your opponents' capabilities. You might categorize each one of them as being aggressive, semi-aggressive, or solid. The best tournament players can read their opponents well enough to play each type differently, even though they have the same type of hand against each one.

At the least, you should be able to look around the table and figure out whether they're playing loose, medium, or tight, and adjust your play to each opponent accordingly. If Joe and Henry are playing loose, you can open up a little bit against them, but don't start playing too loose just because they're loose.

That is an absolute trap. If you're a solid player, you're not accustomed to playing that way. Don't put your money in the way they're playing and expect to get good results right away. Your chances of winning when you play loose against a loose player are about even with their chances of winning, but your results might not turn out 50-50 on a series of hands.

Rather than falling into a trap, let *them* make the play and respond with whatever play you think will either get money or save money. That way you'll find yourself moving up the ladder all the time. And moving up the ladder all the way to the championship is what this book is about.

ALWAYS MAKE QUALITY DECISIONS

In tournament play there are a lot of factors that you cannot control but there also are a lot of things that you *can* control. And you'd better control the factors that you can if you want to get there. You can't control getting your money in with the best hand and losing. But you *can* control putting yourself in risky situations. You don't want to take a flop against a better hand or a better draw and get your money in the middle in a situation that you shouldn't have been in to start with. Some players do that, flop something decent, then get drawn out on, and lose. "I was so unlucky!" they moan.

They weren't unlucky, they played bad or they wouldn't have gotten themselves in that situation in the first place. They were going up against a better hand from the get-go. The idea is to make your opponents have to draw out on you. If they have to draw out on you to win, you have the upper hand, you're in control of the situation.

You always want to try to control your end of every situation. Obviously you can't control what the other players do. You can try to control opponents a little bit by how you bet, but you can't make their decisions for them. But you sure as hell can make your own decisions. When you make your decisions, you should be thinking, "Is this good for me? Is this play going to help increase my stack? Is this going to move me onward?" instead of just jumping right in without thinking about what you're doing.

When you make your plays means a lot in tournaments. If you're playing heads-up in the tournament and you want to make a play at the pot, big deal. You're taking a calculated chance that your opponent will fold. But when you're in fifteenth or sixteenth place, and you still have all those players to go through to win, that's different. The amount of money is so different between those spots and the top spots, you've got to think, "Is this the right play? Do I want to make it *now*?" You have to keep these things in your mind all the time.

People who win tournaments, those who do it consistently, win for a lot of reasons. When it comes down to these kinds of situations, they think it through. With me, I act fast all the time because I don't want anybody to get a tell on me. But believe me, the whole thought process has already gone through my mind. In fact I'm thinking about these things even before they come up. I always think ahead of the play. It's fast for me, but if it takes you a longer time to think it through, take the time to do it.

Take as much time as you need when it's for all your chips. You don't want to take a lot of time for a small amount of chips because you might tip somebody off, have some chips left, and then find your opponent betting at you because he's figured out that you're on a marginal hand. But when it comes down to your tournament life, you've got to take the time to think things through and make the best possible decision.

In summary, before you make your plays, certain thoughts should be going through your head. "Is this a necessary play for me? Am I taking the chance of getting myself knocked out of this tournament or getting crippled because I'm making this play when I don't have to make it for this big an amount of money at this time?"

PART 3

When You're One Table Away From the Money

    The tension builds. Only 36 players are left. You're almost there. Now what?

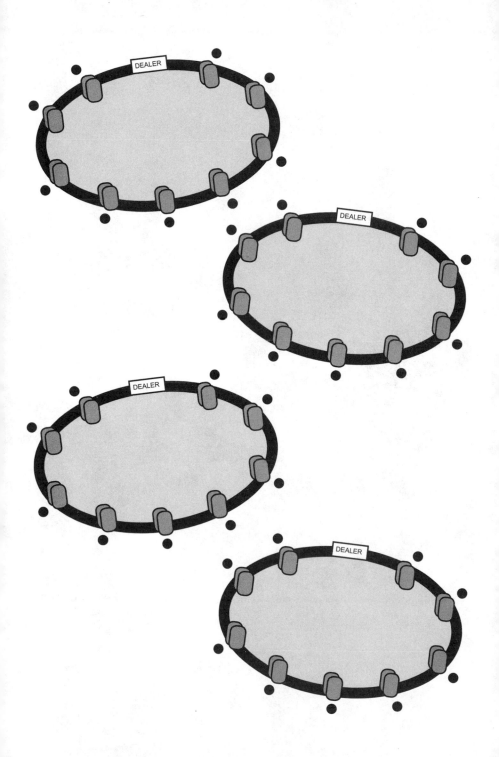

You've been playing no-limit hold'em in a big-field tournament for a couple of days, and now you're just one table away from the money. Only four tables of players are left in the hunt, so you only have to outlast nine more players to make it to the third table where the money is. You want to get there to at least have a payday, but more importantly, if you don't make it to the third table, you won't have a chance to get to the final table where the big money is.

The attitude of this book is that you want to win the tournament. My goal is never to just get into the money. I want to win it all. In this section, I'll talk about how to make it to the money table, but these strategies are not for players who are satisfied with just getting into the money; this advice is for players who want to win the tournament.

For our purposes, you're playing a tournament that pays three tables, 27 players. The following commentary is a discussion of how you might play when you are one table away from the money, when 36 players are still in action. You know that if you don't make it to the money, you have no chance of winning the tournament—and you're somebody who wants to win the whole enchilada.

WHEN YOU HAVE A SMALL STACK

Having a small stack is one thing, but having the smallest stack is something else. If you have the smallest stack at your table, you're just looking for any opportunity to get your money in, and get it in right if you can. You're looking for either the best hand or the best situation. Considerations such as deciding how much to raise have gone out the window. When you make a raise, you have to push your entire stack to the center.

You want to find a hand that you can raise with, and you want to be able to play it for all your chips. Don't put in a portion of your stack and then wind up with an even shorter stack if you lose the hand. You're at the point where you want to play for all your chips. And you want to get them in early in the hand. You're don't want to play a little bit of money here, a little bit there, and then bet the rest of your money on the end if that's the way it comes down.

Suppose you play a hand and you don't get all your money in. There's a little payoff here and a little payoff there, and then your opponents throw their hands away. And you haven't even doubled up on the hand. That makes it tough because all you've accomplished is adding a little bit of chips to your stack, and you still have the antes and blinds to get through. You would like to get your money in with the best hand so that you can double up or even triple up, but the main thing you want to accomplish is getting it all in action and winning.

Your criteria need to be somewhat less than if you were playing with a medium stack or a big stack. Say you're sitting in middle to late position and get dealt an A-10. This type of hand, which you wouldn't play with a bigger stack, suddenly looks pretty good to you. So if you can get A-10 or better in that situation, move in with it because you might not get that good a hand again. Obviously you're taking your chances, but you're the smallest stack at your table anyway, and you need to take a chance to improve your chip position.

Would I move in with two deuces, treys or fours from middle position? No, because I wouldn't want to get called if I moved in with those hands. And I know that with the shortest stack at the table, somebody is going to call my all-in bet. With deuces, treys or fours in that spot, the best you can be is an 11-to-10 favorite, whereas if you have an A-10 you might be an 11-to-10 dog to a pair lower than 10s—but still be the favorite if people call you with a smaller ace or a king-high. If you move in with a small pair, you have to hope that nobody with just two overcards hits one of them. Even against a 6-5, your little pair would be similar to going up against an A-K when you have two queens.

Unless you're just trying to win the blinds without a contest, those baby pairs are dangerous. But that's not the purpose of your play when you're the shortest stack. The idea when you move in is to get called and double up. By going all-in, you know you're going to the river whether or not you hit the flop. You might hit the turn or you might hit the river. But for sure, you're going to see all five cards, and that's the purpose of your all-in bet.

Now let's say that you're sitting in the cut-off position or you're the button. You can raise with a small pair from either of those two spots. You're still taking a big chance with the hand, but you have fewer players sitting behind you who might call. In this case, you're obviously just trying to pick up the blinds. It's late in the tournament, with only 36 players left, and quite a bit of money is sitting out there in the middle.

As for me, I'd just as soon go all in with a 10-9 as I would with a small pair. I know that small pairs are better hands than a 10-9, and I don't want a letter from one of the poker math whizzes telling me how bad an idea this is. My thinking is that when you raise with a baby pair, you might get called by somebody with a 10-9 and lose the hand if they hit one of their overcards.

But when you raise with a hand like 10-9, maybe somebody will call with a low pair and you're only an 11-to-10 dog with your two overcards. It's kind of a reverse action type of thing—you're willing to take a chance because you're short-stacked. I know it may not make a whole lot of sense, but I'm just talking about my personal approach to the game. I'm not saying that I ever would actually raise with a 10-9, I'm just saying that the play is there.

Obviously I like to raise with a decent hand when I put my last money in, but I'm not going to let myself get so short-stacked that it doesn't matter. One more time, let me repeat that I don't want to put my money in, double up, and end up right back where I was before I went through the blinds. That just doesn't make much sense to me. So, I want to go all in with a short stack, and do it as many times as I can, to build some chips. You're going to hold your share of hands—if you're still there to get them. But if you let your stack get too short, you may not be there to get those hands.

Watch Tony Cousineau play a tournament and you can really learn something. He plays a little stack fantastically. When he has a small stack, he lasts forever. And then, all of a sudden, he'll pick up a couple of hands in which a big stack will play with him, and he gets a hold of some chips. He has the right idea about how to play a small stack. And Phil Hellmuth plays a short stack very well. If you had to go down the line and pick one player to last longer than another player at the start of the tournament, Tony and Phil would be two of the guys you'd want to pick.

WHEN YOU HAVE A MEDIUM STACK

Playing a medium stack requires a different approach than when you have a short stack, where you want to pick it up all at one time. When I'm an average stack, I don't want to lose even one pot unless I have a premium hand that gets drawn out on. I want to pick up a little here, a little there, a little more here and there, and all of a sudden, I become a large stack.

A medium stack is the average on the curve, so you're right where you should be. When you have an average stack, you're going to play cards. You don't play any differently when 36 players are left than you have played all along, unless you notice different situations from the small stacks. You don't want to let them see daylight. You might work the small stacks when you have a medium stack, but you definitely are not attacking the big stacks without a premium hand.

The idea is to stay away from the big stacks. I don't want to play against large stacks that are willing to take chances against me because they can wipe me out in one hand. Attack the small stacks or the other medium stacks but, preferably, the small stacks. All the while, continue to play solid poker. When I say "solid," I don't mean that you should be looking for aces or kings before you play a hand. Look for situations where you can get your money in when you believe you have the best hand.

WHEN YOU HAVE A BIG STACK

With a large stack, you want to attack the small stacks. You want to play against the medium stacks when you have premium hands. And you want to play the other big stacks when you have an A-Number-1 hand. You don't want to put yourself in jeopardy. A big stack is worth preserving. You have enough chips to move on, so why not give yourself a chance to do that?

I've seen players make more mistakes with big stacks than with any other size of stack. They get in a hurry and want to win the tournament right there. Some players become what I call "chip happy." They've played pretty good poker all day, or have gotten lucky early and then started playing good poker. They've gotten a hold of a lot of chips and have a big stack in front of them. Then they get real close to the money, and suddenly they start playing every pot and believing they can win them all. And it doesn't work. I saw one of the greatest hold'em players of all time, Stu Ungar, playing in a $10,000 buy-in tournament at the Nugget years ago. With three tables to go, he had a third of the chips in play—a third of the chips! But he was in one of those moods that he got into once in a while where he played every pot and stood every raise with any two cards, just trying to take somebody off a hand. And guess what? He did not make it to two tables!

Don't alter the way you've been playing all along.

That kind of play is what got you your chips. But stay away from all trap hands and all drawing hands. Sometimes it's tough to know where the traps are. When I say "traps," I mean standing raises with hands like K-Q, K-J, Q-J, Q-10 and J-10. A-J and A-10 are trap hands, too. Actually, J-10 is better than most of these trap hands, not because it's a better hand, but because sometimes it's a better hand to play against another hand. You always need a 10 or 5 to make a straight, plus the fact that the guys playing against you usually don't have those cards, meaning that they're live cards. Obviously if your opponent has a K-J and you have a J-10, you're a big dog to the hand. But if he has A-K or A-Q, you're only about a 2 to 1 dog to the hand. It may sound strange, I know, but if he has one of your cards, you understand that one of your cards is out of play, and you're a big dog unless you make two pair or a straight with the hand.

A lot of players get a hold of a big stack and start playing these trap hands and becoming overly aggressive in their play. And pretty soon, guess what? They don't have a big stack any more. The guys who have the medium stacks, and are playing correctly, are just looking for opportunities to take some chips from a big stack that is gambling with mediocre hands. You don't want to be the one who starts giving away your hard-earned chips by playing those sorry-looking hands.

The point is that you don't have to be in a hurry

with your big stack. Suppose you have $100,000 in your stack and the blinds are $1,000-$2,000 with a $300 ante. It will cost you $5,700 to play a round. This means that you have enough chips to play 17 or 18 rounds. Why rush your play? Now let's say that you have $100,000 and the blinds will increase in five minutes to $1,500-$3,000 with an ante of $500. In that case, it will cost you $9,000 to play a round, which means that you still have enough chips to play 11 rounds. Even then, why rush?

Stay focused on looking for premium cards and premium situations when you're playing nine, eight, or seven-handed. Play the kind of game that got you the big stack, except avoid the drawing hands. Suppose you've called a raise with the K♣ J♣, the flop comes with the Q♣ 10♣, and you make your hand on the river. Just because you've done it once doesn't mean you can do it twice. You say to yourself, "Anybody in the world's gonna play K♣ J♣ when the Q♣ 10♣ is out there." True, but not everybody in the world is going to stand a raise to see that flop. Consider yourself lucky to have gotten there with it one time and make a note to yourself not to try it again. Lightning might not strike twice.

Here's something to take note of regarding the incremental increases in the blinds and antes. Not all tournaments increase the blinds gradually with 50 percent increases at the start of each new round. Some of them double the increments every round, especially in the smaller buy-in events. Further, in almost all tournaments that start each new level with an increase of 50 percent, the blinds double in the late rounds. This usually happens at a particular level.

For example, suppose the blinds increase from $1,500-$3,000 and then $2,000-$4,000, followed by $3,000-$6,000, and $5,000-$10,000. In many big buy-in events, they start doubling after that, increasing from $5,000-$10,000 to $10,000-$20,000, then to $20,000-$40,000 and so on. If you are one of the chip leaders, you like it when the increases start to double. But if you are a medium stack or a short stack, in particular, you don't like it. The big stacks have the advantage when the blinds double every round because the small stacks are forced to come into pots with marginal hands that they don't want to play. And that gives the big stacks an edge.

With a big stack, you want to increase your chips as you go along, but the main thing is that you don't want to lose any of them. You want to get to the money, and then start moving a little more as you get closer and closer to the bigger money. Just remember that anybody who wins a tournament has gotten lucky at some point along the way. You might've gotten lucky earlier in the tournament getting a hold of that big stack, but don't count on getting lucky again. I've seen it happen, yes, but I've seen times when luck turns against you. And there's not a thing you can do about it when that happens.

PART 4

When You've Made It to the First Money Table

Now there are only 27 players left. You've reached your first goal on your way to the top—you are in the money.

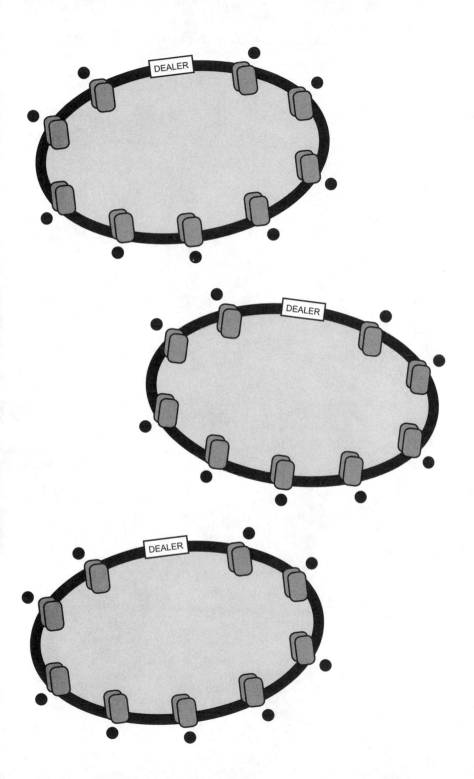

When the action gets down to three tables, which is where the money starts in our example, everybody redraws for a new seat assignment. In an ideal redraw, if there are nine shorter stacks, they will be evenly distributed with about three short stacks at each table. Sometimes, however, the redraw puts most of the long money at one table, and most of the short money is at one table.

Once you get to the third table, the table that pays everybody the same amount of money, it's incredible how fast things move before you get to two tables. It's very slow-going getting to the first money table, but once you make it to the money it's the fastest part of the whole tournament. Everybody has worried about tightening up to make the money, and then all of a sudden, they just loosen up and start playing any two cards. Since there are a lot of chips in play, even the short stacks have money so they open up their games. They're going to gamble, but sometimes they do more gambling than they need to. Be very guarded about playing that way yourself; don't open up too much.

You still have to play good poker to get to the real money.

After you redraw at 27 players, your first order of business is to find out how everybody plays, what category they fall in to. And do it in a hurry. Then use that knowledge to your advantage.

Some players also like to find out what the next money increment is. For example, players who place 27th through 19th usually receive the same amount of prize money. Places 18, 17, and 16 get paid a little more; spots 15, 14, and 13 receive a bigger payout; places 12 and 11 get more, and spot 10 (often called the "bubble" when nine players go to the final table) receives a bonus. Knowing that everybody at the initial money table gets paid the same amount, a lot of players move into a maniac mode trying to pick up chips and move ahead of the pack.

Conversely, a few timid souls start playing tight-conservative poker just hoping they'll be able to inch up to the next money level. You don't have to use either of these styles to move up the money ladder. Just stay with the solid-aggressive game that probably got you to the money in the first place.

WHEN YOU HAVE A SHORT STACK

The short stacks are going to gamble after the redraw. They've made the money and now all of a sudden, two deuces or treys or fours look good to them. They're not worth the paint it took to put them on the cards (unless you flop three of them), but those small pairs look good to some short stacks because they're in the money now. They're not thinking about winning the tournament. They're thinking about getting their money in and, if they get lucky and their small pairs hold up, fine. But they're not really looking at the overall picture.

As a short stack, you should be aware that this is happening, that the other short stacks will move in their whole stacks right away. And they do it from any position, which is what really throws me. They might look down at an A-8 in first position and boom—it all goes in! They forget that there are eight players sitting behind them who could have a bigger hand. If they get called, it's almost certain that their hand is beaten already, and they're going to have to draw out to win the pot. With those kinds of odds, it's a foolish play if you think about it. But people don't think about it. This is why there's so much movement and so many players going out at this stage.

A lot of players gauge their play according to the number of big blinds they have left in their stack. For example, a buddy of mine who is an excellent middle-limit tournament player, says that if he's in the money with three to five times the amount of the big blind, he's ready to play. And if he only has four times the big blind, he's definitely moving in while he still has some leverage. I realize that this type of math works for some players, but I don't think that way.

When I'm short-stacked, I'm just looking for "the" hand to play. To put it another way, whereas a lot of analytical players compare their stacks to the size of the blinds, I am an intuitive player who relies heavily on my instincts. I don't consciously think of the math, although the math is always there and I understand it very well.

If I am very short-stacked at this stage, I'm not going to be doing a lot of gambling, but I am going to try to increase my chips somehow. I'm going to take a chance here and take a chance there. But it's going to be a calculated risk, a measured chance, instead of just putting in my chips the first time I see two cards that I like.

Even with the blinds coming, I'm not moving in with hands like K-7 or Q-4 from the first seat. I'd rather take my chances with a random hand in the blind. I might make a move with a trouble hand such as K-Q or K-J, but not with a Q-6 suited, for example. A lot of players like to play two suited cards, but they usually wind up singing what I call a broke's lament: "I went out with J-7, but I was suited." With a short stack at the third table, you still have to play good poker.

WHEN YOU HAVE A MEDIUM TO LARGE STACK

If you have a medium to large stack, you know that the short stacks are going to be playing looser, playing lots of hands. A guy who wouldn't call a raise with an A-10 suddenly puts in his whole stack with a K-10 or a Q-10. "I'm in the money now, I'm gonna get my chips in action," players like that are thinking. "I've done what I'm supposed to do, now let's go!"

But that's not the way to play things. If you play smart, you can be the recipient of at least some of their money. Take advantage of this situation, but keep in mind that there are going to be a lot of draw-outs at this point, because players tend to put their money in quickly. You want to be the raiser, not the caller. And you certainly don't want to call unless you have a premium hand, not two cards such as A-J offsuit. You want to dictate the action, not follow it. Remember my old axiom, "A bettor be, a caller never be."

You'll also see some medium stacks playing too loose. Maybe they've gotten there by drawing out on their opponents and now all of a sudden they open up too. You have all the opportunities in the world to get a hold of money when you just get to that 27-player bracket of the tournament. If you play good cards right there, you can get a hold of a lot of chips.

Almost invariably, it's those times from 36 to 27, and 27 to 18, when I usually get a hold of most of my chips. If I start with an average stack, that average stack becomes a better stack. That's where I try to get some chips because of the situations that are going on. I pick out the players that are doing such-and-such, notice when they're doing it, and use my observation powers and instincts to get the chips. I know that when there are two tables to go, it gets a lot tougher so I want to get the chips while I can.

When we're one table out of the money, everybody's playing pretty conservatively. And that's when I'm going to open up a little and take some of that money. Then when I get to the third money table, I really open up. "But the other guys are opening up, too, aren't they?" I've been asked. Actually, I shouldn't say that I'm opening up—the short stacks are opening up and making the opportunities for me to get the money. I play well enough that I can see who's doing what, so that I'm going to win with hands that are a little weaker than I normally would play. Even though I believe that I have the best hand, it might be a hand that I wouldn't have played against them early on. But now that I know the situation, I can play those hands for a profit.

The situations where I'm going to make a move against the short stacks depend on my position at the table. Sometimes the short stacks move in from the cutoff seat or on the button, but they usually move in when they're getting close to having to post the blinds. Say that a small stack is going to get the big blind on the next hand dealt, or the hand before that, that is, the first two seats before the blinds get to him.

Almost invariably, they make their move at that point, and they often make it with a lot weaker hand than they would have played if the blinds hadn't been coming. You'll see these guys moving in with K-7, Q-4, some crazy hands, because they don't want to have to put their money in from the blinds.

Suppose you're sitting around the backside with a medium to large stack where you don't figure you're going to get reraised; that is, you're in a spot where you're not likely to get yourself into trouble with a hand. You pick up K-Q or K-J. Now it's not a trouble hand any more, it's a playable hand, a hand that can take out one of those little stacks that are gambling.

You can't do it every time, of course; you have to pick your spots. Just remember that when you're playing less than A-1 premium hands, you have to be in the right position to make these calls so that you don't get yourself in real trouble. Of course, the short stacks have as good a chance to wake up with a real hand as anybody else. But a situation usually will arise where they're making a move because the blinds are about to eat them up, and they'd rather go in with a high card and a bad kicker than a random hand they might catch in the blind.

There usually are enough small stacks below par that it doesn't behoove the medium stacks to gamble because they're going to move up in the money anyway if the little stacks get knocked out. With a medium stack, you play poker. You take advantage of the small stacks when you're in position to take it. The key is being in position, so that you aren't leaving yourself open to a big stack or a stack equal to your size to take you off. That's why you want to make sure you're around back so you won't get rehashed. Say that the small stack moves in with something like K-8, and you have a K-Q or K-J. You want to make sure that there's nobody behind you that will re-pop you when you make the call.

WHEN YOU HAVE A LARGE STACK

If you have a big stack, your goal is to win every pot you play—period. Somebody asked me, "How did you get a hold of your chips, TJ? You don't play very many pots." I answered, "I try to win the ones I play." If that's your goal throughout the whole tournament, it's a pretty good thought process. You have to win the pots you play. And if you do, you're going to get a hold of plenty of chips. And when you have a big stack at the third table, you definitely want to be sure that you have a good enough hand to win the pots you play. You didn't work all day long to get a big stack and then give it away once you get to the money. That doesn't make sense. When you have a big stack, you have enough chips to play at the final table, so make sure you get there. Of course you might take a bad beat, but there's nothing you can do about that anyway.

"Aren't the big stacks at the other tables muscling the short stacks and helping you climb up the money ladder?" I've been asked. That depends on who has the big stacks. The good players will muscle in certain spots, but they're not going to muscle when they're out of position. "I have a big stack now," good players say to themselves, "but if I muscle up this average stack and he wins the pot, he's gonna be a big stack and I'll be back to average."

So, when it comes to muscling other players, you can muscle the short stacks because they are at an absolute disadvantage unless they hold good hands to start with. But be sure you have something when you do it. There's no reason for you to over-gamble when you have a big-big stack with three tables to go. In addition to the short stacks that are gambling, you'll find some of the medium-stack players also are firing it up, usually because they don't know any better. You have to watch out for them, too. Invariably a couple of them are going to draw out on somebody. Hopefully, it won't be you. Try to have the best hand, especially if you're in a pot with someone who has equal chips or more.

Some players with big stacks have heard the myth that it's their job to knock out the little stacks. You know what my job in a poker tournament is? To knock the last player out. Period. I don't care whether I knock anybody else out. You might, but it isn't necessary. When I say that I open up a little more when we get to the last three tables, I mean that I take advantage of the guys who are moving with the small stacks. I don't really open up my play to the point where I could get destroyed.

You don't want to have a big stack, one that already

would be an average stack at the final table, and blow your money in bad spots. Remember that if all you win is the antes and blinds during each round of the table, you've won a free round. And if you win one raised pot per round, you've probably won four rounds of the table. So if you just play poker—*real* poker—you've got a chance to win it all. But if you don't, if you get in a hurry and try to win the tournament too early, or if you try to over-attack people with hands that you should not be playing, invariably you're a goner.

PART 5

When You've Made It to the Second Money Table

You're only one table away from the final table. With 18 players left, you've reached your second goal in the tournament. If you can just make it through nine more players, you'll have a shot at the title.

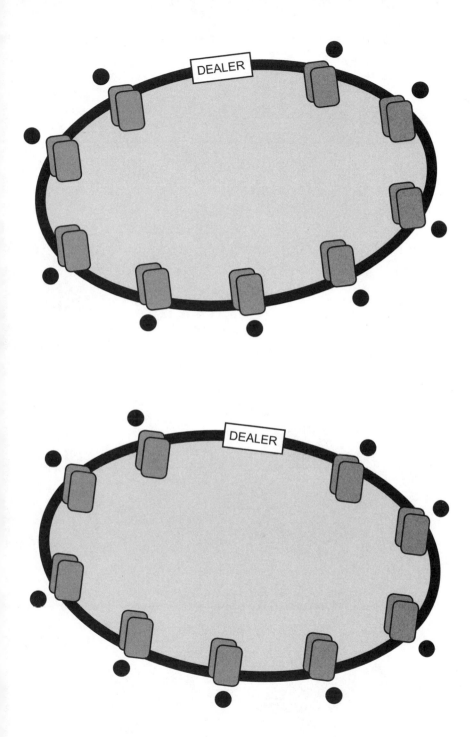

Now we're down to two tables, 18 players in our example of a tournament that pays the final three tables (27 players).

Whereas the third money table usually is the fastest moving part of the tournament, the second table is slow, slow, slow. At the WSOP in 1985, when I came in second to Bill Smith, we played five and a half hours just to get from 10 players to 9 players. Bill was all in four or five times, and every time he had A-K and he was up against A-K, and every time they split the pot. He was the shortest stack at the second table, but by the time we got to the final table he had built up his stack pretty well. This is just an example of how slowly the second table can move.

A lot of chips are out, and there is a lot of play to the second table. Everybody will be playing pretty conservatively at the start of the second money table with a full ring of nine players at each table. They aren't really going to start swinging until it gets a little shorthanded, with six players at each table or six at one and five at the other. That's when you'll start seeing some play, and that's when you'll have to show them a hand.

The only exception is when a player like Layne Flack, Scott Fischman or John Phan is at your table; in other words, very aggressive players that don't miss playing very many hands. They may try to seize the situation and really start moving chips early. If that happens, my suggestion is to play your own game. Just because they're moving around a lot doesn't mean that you have to. Invariably these overly aggressive players are going to knock some players out, or get knocked out themselves, with their aggressive style of play. They're trying to garner all the chips right then.

Actually they start playing this way from the very beginning. They don't play to the situation, they play to their own style of poker more than to situations. So when you have one of these players or one of their clones at your table, don't let it affect your play. You should still be playing premium hands. So what if they steal a few pots here and there? That isn't going to affect you much. You're still going to hold your share of the hands, and when you do, maybe you can take them off.

There may be one or two short stacks, but in general, everyone has chips. Every now and then, you'll see a tournament where someone has a ton of chips and absolutely dominates the tournament, but that really should not affect your play when you're at 18 players. Even if one guy has a ton of chips, remember that if he loses a few pots and you win a few pots, all of a sudden you're back on equal terms.

If you have a small stack when 18 players are left, it's a little harder to push it through because, usually, there are very few small stacks and a lot of medium to large stacks. So, you're at a point where you need to have some kind of a hand if you want to make a move. Or hope that you get lucky. It isn't just a question of getting away with making a move when people are already in the money and are starting to get close to the serious money. They're going to play hands at this point. So, until you get short-handed, you don't think about making very many moves.

When you get short-handed, there are lots of moves you can make. Now a lot of the "bunching" theories of cards and other ideas like that go out the door because you're playing five or six-handed. When you're playing nine-handed, the bunching theory is that if the first six players don't have anything, it's likely that the last three players do have a hand because of the number of cards that are out. But when you're playing 5-handed, only 10 cards out of 52 are out.

So it isn't necessarily true that if the first two players pass and you want to make a move on the pot from the middle, that the two players left to act behind will have hands, because there are still so many cards left in the deck. So, obviously, your chances of picking up the pot in short-handed games are greater than they are in long-handed games.

Certain kinds of hands increase in value in short-handed play. For example, unless someone raises in front of you, a hand like A-10 has some value, whereas it wouldn't have had much value nine-handed. The trouble hands such as K-Q, K-J, or K-10 have some value from the button in, that is, from the button, the small blind, and the big blind. I don't give them much value from up front.

Suppose you are in the small blind with something like K-Q or K-J. Everyone, including the button, passes to you. You can play the hand, even though you will have to act first after the flop. If you decide to raise with it, the big blind will not call a great percentage of the time. But even if he does, you don't necessarily have the worst hand; in fact, in short-handed action, you probably have the best hand. Players in the big blind often will call raises with cards such as J-10, 10-9, Q-J, or K-anything. And they'll play any ace— that is, an ace with a bad kicker—like it's the holy city.

As for me, I need to have a kicker when I have an ace. I just can't force myself to play an ace without a kicker, although sometimes I do play an A-5. But A-6, A-7, A-8—those hands can get you into trouble. An ace with a wheel card is stronger that an ace with a middle card because of its potential to make a straight—unless, of course, you're up against an ace with a bigger kicker. They don't come up too often, but they do come up. Stu Ungar's winning hand in the

1997 WSOP is a good example of making a straight with an ace-wheel-card hand. In his comeback victory, Stu played an A-4 offsuit head-up against John Strzemp's A-8 offsuit. When the flop came A-5-3, John bet $12,000, Ungar moved all in with the chip lead, and John called with his case chips. The board paired threes on the turn but the river card was a deuce, giving Stu the winning wheel.

Players redraw for seat assignments at the start of two-table play so, as soon as you get to your new table, you must identify the types of players at the table. And do it in a hurry. The absolutely first criterion when you move to a new table is to get to know your opponents. Learn who is capable of doing what in which situations, and identify who you can do what against. Then take it to the next level by asking yourself, "How are they playing today?" You might remember how Joe plays from playing with him previously, but how is he playing right now? Is he following his usual pattern, or is he mixing it up? Does he seem to be off his game? Certain players change their styles of play, while others are just so cut and dried that they play the same way every time.

You have to play every player individually. Unless you're capable of doing this—you play this guy one way, that guy another way, the next guy some other way—you might win once in a while, but you're not going to win very often. You might know all the players at your new table, and the chances are good that you'll at least know some of them. So you'll want to put your attention in the beginning on the players you haven't played against.

At the start of two-table action when you're playing in a full ring, expect that you're going to have to play poker, real poker. You're going to have to show them a hand. Even if you just have an average stack, you have enough chips to play with. For the first time in the tournament, you can really play poker because you have plenty of chips to play with, even though the antes and blinds are high. You'll hear a lot of tournament players complaining about the blinds being too high to play poker. But that mostly applies to smaller buy-in events with short fields and shorter rounds, where poker becomes a showdown game. In big buy-in tournaments with big fields, there are plenty of chips to play with.

You can start opening up your game at six-handed play. Now you start attacking some stacks and try to accumulate chips. Keep in mind that the jump in prize money from tenth place to ninth place is hardly anything. Until you get to three places in almost any tournament, you're not into the real money. So, you can make some moves as you go along since the prize-money jumps don't go up that high, unless you're in a huge buy-in tournament where the difference in jumps is $100,000 or so.

You have to be willing to open up and play a little bit. You have to formulate a plan based on who you're playing with. When you get to two tables and you're in a full ring, you start formulating your plan *then* for when you're playing short-handed at that same table. Every once in a while, they'll throw a monkey wrench at you and switch you over to the other table. For example, the other table has lost two players and your table is still full, so they move somebody to even up the tables. In that case, you have to start all over again, but you just go through the same process at the other table.

I start formulating my plan of attack when I first hit the table. In fact, I do that subconsciously from day one.

THE TABLE-TWO PLAN
With a Big Stack

Obviously you want to stay away from attacking the big stacks. Even if you have a big stack yourself, you don't want to attack the other big stacks unless you're sitting there with the stone nuts because a big stack can knock you out. If you're going to attack anybody, attack the smaller stacks. Generally, the small stacks will be looking to get into action and they will create it for you. Let them do that. Let them come to you. Let them create the action. Of course if you have great hands, you're going to play them at any point throughout the tournament.

Ask yourself, "What can I do at this table to make sure that I get to the next table?" Number one, you say to yourself, "I don't need any confrontations with mediocre hands with my big stack against another big stack." Because if you're wrong, you're gone! And I don't think you want to be in that situation. Any time that you have a big stack and you're going against an average stack—and you lose—all of a sudden, they're a big stack and you're an average stack. They'll chop you right in half. So use the same type of play with them. You just want to play real, real solid and let the other players knock themselves out. That's usually my plan at two tables when I have an average stack or larger.

Then I'm going to open up, just like I've said before, when we get short-handed. Everybody's trying to get to that final table and they're playing a little close, so you can steal some blinds, and rob some raises by going back over the top of the raiser. But you have to pick your spots pretty well. When you try to steal or rob, you don't do it for all your chips. That's where people make their biggest mistakes. They think that when they're trying to steal this pot or rob that blind, they have to put in their whole stack to do it. You don't have to do that. You *can* send a boy out there once in a while instead of a man.

Say that you're sitting there with $100,000 in chips and somebody makes it $7,000 to go, the standard raise. If you want to take it away from him, you could probably do it for a $10,000 to $15,000 raise just as easy as you could for all your chips. If your opponent will call that amount of raise, he'll call for the rest of your chips. And then you're in jeopardy. So, if you're going to make a play at the pot, be smart about how you do it. Don't fall into the trap that a lot of tournament players do—don't move in every time you raise. If you move in every time you raise, sooner or later you'll get chopped off, and then you're gone.

The amount that you reraise depends on who your opponent is and the size of your stack. Make a raise that is big enough to hurt him if he calls, but small enough that it won't hurt you if he calls and wins the pot. Let's look at a scenario when you're trying to take a pot away from a player. In this example, the blinds are $1,000-$2,000 with a $300 ante. Suppose he makes it $8,000 to go, and you raise him to $24,000. You have a lot of chips, so the amount of your raise will still leave you with plenty of chips. In this example, you *don't* have a hand, you're just trying to steal the pot.

This formula is also a pretty good one when you do have a hand. Say that you're playing six-handed or shorter, and a player raises it $8,000. You have pocket queens and decide to reraise him. If you make it $24,000 more and he comes back over the top for all his chips, you can still get away from the hand. But if you make a raise of $60,000 more, you're not going to be able to get away from it—now you're going to play. And if he comes back over the top in this spot, he probably has aces or kings.

You'll hear tournament commentators say that a player made a pot-size raise, or that he raised four times the big blind. I don't think about raising in those terms. What I try to do is make the size of raise that I figure my opponent will call—or won't call. It all depends on what I want him to do. For example, if there's $16,000 in the pot, I don't want to make a small bet when I have a big hand. My small bet might just tip off an opponent that I want him to call, and therefore cause him to fold. I'll make a bet that I think he will call. I've seen players who bet small with big hands, and bet big with small hands. How smart is that?! Tailor your bet according to what you want your opponent to do, not to the strength of your hand.

I made a mistake in a tournament in a hand that I could have played differently and that would have resulted in a better outcome for me. The situation came up during the second day of the $25K buy-in WPT championship tournament at the Bellagio. The blinds were $400-$800 with a $100 ante. I was on the button with an A-6 and it was passed to me. I made a standard raise of $1,800 and David Chiu in the big blind reraised me $6,000.

Acting quickly, I moved all-in for $60,000 thinking that he had two nines, tens or jacks and would lay them down against a monster raise. My mistake was in the amount that I reraised. My reraise was so huge that it stunk like a bluff. If I had reraised $20,000, it would have looked like I had a much stronger hand, especially to a good player like David, who probably would have released his hand. He called and turned over pocket jacks. As a result of this play, I was knocked out of the tournament.

You're not going to be right every time you make a move, but you can be smart every time you make a move. This is why I suggest that making a raise that is about triple your opponent's bet is plenty to reraise. Of course you can't be doing this when you have short chips or a medium stack. You make these plays when you have a large stack. This is one of the ways you build your stack. Even though you have a large stack, you build it into a larger stack. I've used this strategy for years.

I don't usually move in on them. But if I do move in, I do it against a guy that I think will call my move-in bet—and only when I have the hand I want to have, aces or kings. I don't have a 4-3 or something like that, because if I get called, I want to have the best hand. The idea of the reraise is to get the money right then, not to play the pot out.

The point is that when you have a big stack, you're looking to build it even higher without putting your entire stack in jeopardy all at one time. Any time you put yourself in jeopardy for all your chips, you have to do it with cards that you believe are the best hand. Your instincts and observations will guide you. Making an out-and-out bluff for all your chips is fine, if you want to do that. But if you get called, you'd better have some great suck-out power.

When you have a big stack, don't get involved with hands that will tear your stack apart. For example, I don't want to get involved when a player has raised and I'm looking down at a small pair. Or, suppose it's shorthanded and you're in the small blind or the big blind. A short stack moves in. I think one of the worst things that players do in this spot is figure that they have to be the policeman; that is, they have to call with any two cards.

If you do that two or three times and lose, your stack will dwindle while the short stack catches up to par. It's different if you're sitting there in the big blind with $500,000 in chips and somebody moves in for $25,000. In that case, you have a chance to knock him out. But when you have a decent sized stack and the short stack moves in with enough to do some damage to your stack, you don't call the raise with any two cards. That would be ridiculous.

Treat that blind money you have in the pot as though it isn't your money, so that it isn't something that you have to protect. You're out of position on any hand you play from the blinds anyway. If you can do that successfully, you will do a lot better in tournament play. People who protect their blinds routinely, especially in short-handed play when you're getting down to where it counts, are just looking to burn up their chips.

Say you have $400,000 and the short stack has

$30,000 and he pushes it all in. You have a $1,600 blind already in the pot. You have to put in $28,400 more to call the raise. "I've got $400,000," you think, "so it won't hurt me at all to call." That's baloney. If you don't have a hand, don't do it. Follow your regular playing criteria.

Now suppose you have $400,000 with $1,600 already in the pot, and the short stack moves in with his last $4,000. If you want to call him, fine. It's only $2,400 more, not $28,400. A lot of times at this stage, the short stacks still have a formidable amount of chips, and they can do a lot of damage to your stack. If you call three times and lose against somebody who has $30,000 in chips, $90,000 of your chips will be gone. And you know you're taking the worst of it to start with every time. To me, that's foolish, yet you see it happen all the time.

Another bad play is one that I've seen happen at the final table as well as at the second table. It's passed to the button and the button has a lot of chips, so he tries to steal the pot. I watched a tournament where "Joe" had a 9-3 offsuit on the button and tried to steal the pot against the blinds. At the time he had the second largest stack at the table with the small blind sitting behind him on a much shorter stack. The small blind studied and studied and finally moved in for all his chips. He already had $1,600 in the pot and it cost him his remaining $4,000 chips to just call. The big blind folded. Joe called.

Joe had made his move at the pot with a 9-3, so why didn't he just give it up? Apparently he felt obligated to make the call and lost his chips when the small blind showed him pocket queens. This loss put him into a bad frame of mind. The next two times he had the button, Joe had a K-10 each time. When it was passed to him, he made big raises, and lost both times to better hands. I think that if Joe hadn't lost so much the first time he tried to steal the blinds with a 9-3, he probably wouldn't have followed through with the two K-10 hands and lost that money. By the way, Joe went out seventh in the tournament and the short stack, who had been the shortest stack at the start of the final table, lasted all the way to third place.

Nothing was wrong with the first part of Joe's button play, trying to steal the blinds. But once he got played with, why compound things and lose more chips to the hand? I think that's a cardinal sin. If you do that two or three times, suddenly you're a short stack. If somebody plays back at you when you're on a steal, give up the steal-money you have in the pot. Certainly you shouldn't try a steal by pushing in your whole stack. Raise enough to make it a formidable call, but be willing to give it up if you get played with.

When you raise from the cutoff seat or on the button, realize that your raise may force the short stacks to play. If the short stack is in one of the blinds with only a few chips left in his stack, he's going to play just about any two cards. You've given him a reason to call. (You might have a hand on the button, of course.) When it's passed to the button, the blinds expect the button to raise. Even Joe Blow from Idaho is smart enough to know that the button has position on him and is going to try to take advantage of him before the flop. So, they expect the raise. And while everybody's been passing, they've had time to work their nerve to call.

To recap, your goal with a big stack at the second table is number one, to build it, and number two, to preserve it. And don't take too many risks by sending in too many soldiers at one time. Make decent raises, but don't go for all of it. Avoid confrontations with other big stacks and with medium stacks. Unless you have a big hand, you only want to play the short stacks because they have to play with marginal hands. You don't want to lose any big confrontations where you can lose a lot of chips. Your goal is still to get to the final table. And once you get there, your goal is to win.

With a Medium Stack

It's a little tougher to get a hold on how to play a medium stack than it is to explain how to play a big stack and a small stack. A medium stack, they say, is the toughest size of stack to play. You're forced to play a small stack and you don't have as much pressure when you have a big stack—you have some leisure to play it (so long as you don't play it badly). With a medium stack, you're right where you're *supposed* to be in the tournament—that is, you have an average stack—but you're not where you *want* to be. You want to have a lot of chips. If twelve players are left, there might be three big stacks, six medium stacks, and three short stacks. You want to be one of those three big stacks, but how do you get there?

When you're playing short-handed and you have a medium stack, you're looking for some hands to play because you want to have some chips when you get to the final table. Yet you're being selective about the hands you play because with average chips, you still have plenty. Why get in a hurry? You don't have to rush. Let the cards come to you. Let the flow come your way.

If I have a medium stack, I'm looking for opportunities to get a hold of some chips, but I'm still playing good poker. I'm playing two tens or higher pretty strong, and I'm still playing a big ace pretty strong. I'm making raises with these hands, but I'm not usually moving in with them. I want to see a flop. I want to know where I'm at after some cards are out there.

In certain situations, however, I might move in. Say that somebody comes in for a raise and he has fewer chips than me. If I have A-K and decide to play the hand, I might move in, trying to get all their chips in the pot. Of course A-K is always a "decision" hand. Preferably you don't move in with the hand against somebody who can break you, but there are situations where you will, where you'll take the coin flip. But let's face it, you have to win the coin flips in tournament poker. You have to win both sides of them. I went out of a tournament recently because I lost both coin flips I played. I had A-K against two fives, and I had two queens against A-K, and I lost both sides of it. When that happens to you, you're a goner.

The hands that players have a lot of problems with are hands like A-Q and A-J. If they get a big play with these hands, they're usually the underdog. That A-Q against A-K is a big underdog. And A-J against A-Q is a big underdog. But when you're playing short-handed, all of a sudden those hands look pretty good. And they are pretty good—they're a lot better than an average hand. The so-called "computer hand" was Q-7. The reason the computer chose the Q-7 was because it determined that it is the "average" or medium hand that is dealt, not because it was a good hand.

To recap, you're looking for hands to play when you're a medium stack, but you still have to be pretty selective with them. You know the players at your table, you know what they're doing. If you have two jacks and the flop comes 10-high, how are you going to play the hand? You've raised before the flop and now you lead at it. If you get played with, then what do you do? Have you put your opponent on a 10, an underpair, or does he have you beaten with an overpair? This is not a situation where I can tell you what to do. This is where your poker skills have to come into play. I can't tell you what to do, you just have to know what to do.

Don't ever think that somebody won't just flat-call a raise with two queens before the flop because a lot of players will do just that. You should have that type of player identified so that when you raise with two jacks before the flop and somebody calls, you know what cards he's most likely to call with. Does he call raises with small pairs? Does he call raises with A-K, A-Q, A-J, or A-10? With suited connectors? Exactly how does he play? If you know that he plays all these types of hands, and the flop comes 10-high, you're going to lead at the hand anyway with two jacks. But if you have a little buzz in your brain that warns you he might be slow-playing something, be ready to shut down and give it up. If that isn't your first instinct, you'd better lead at the pot because it is very likely that you can win the pot right there.

Just remember that all you have is one pair. A lot of people get broke with kings or queens on the flop, or on fourth or fifth street. But after it's all said and done, they only had one pair, they didn't have a big hand that got beaten. Sure, it might have started out being a big hand, like aces or kings, but still all they can beat is one pair. The flop might come 5-4-3 or 8-7-6 or three of a suit, and their opponent makes a straight or flush to beat them. Or the board might be showing a jack and a 10, and somebody has two oddball cards like J-10 in his hand. Or the flop comes 10-high and then an ace hits on the turn. A lot of people play A-10.

You have to be willing to get away from one pair if you want to save your life in a poker tournament. I don't mean just on the road to the final table, I mean all the way through a tournament. It's tough to do when you've raised going in with a big pocket pair, but boy, you'd better be right when you put in all your money with one pair after there has been some play to the hand—that is, on the flop, turn or river.

Also be aware that a lot of former limit-hold'em players are playing no-limit hold'em. Because the bets in limit hold'em are limited to a certain size, players can only lose that size of bet (if they aren't raised). So, a lot of times, limit hold'em players will call a bet on the flop to see what comes off on fourth street. They often carry over this play into no-limit tournaments.

They tend to forget that in no-limit hold'em, you have to call various sizes of bets to see the turn card, so it can cost them a lot more money. For example, if you have $100 in the pot and you have to call $400 to see the next card, that's a little tougher than if you only have to call another $100 to see it. Just be aware that if you're playing against someone who usually plays limit hold'em, they are likely to be willing to pay to see the turn card if they believe they have a good chance of winning the pot. They often will call on the flop with a lone ace and no pair to see the turn card. In fact when you're categorizing the players at your table, add "limit player" to your list.

Since you're trying to get a hold of some chips, you're going to be aggressive in spots, particularly when the situation allows you to be aggressive. If you're playing six-handed and three players have passed to you, you might decide to play J-10 from around back. There's nothing wrong with making a play with J-10 in this spot because you actually might have the best hand anyway. You have to vary your play. You can't let your opponents pigeonhole you as somebody who only plays A-B-C. But I wouldn't make a big habit of doing it. You have to make a play once in a while to at least keep the status quo, or increase your stack a little bit.

Give yourself a chance to win. By giving yourself a chance to win, I mean that you have enough patience to wait for a hand, and you seize every situation that comes up in your favor. Usually you wouldn't play the trouble hands when you have a medium stack, but in short-handed play those trouble hands go up in value. When you're sitting around back at a short-handed table and you have K-Q, that K-Q has a lot more value than it had when you were playing nine-handed. This is because the more cards that are dealt, more hands can be out against you.

Of course everybody who plays goes through what we call "dead spots." If you don't run into any dead spots, you're gonna walk off with everything. Layne

Flack did this in a tournament where he had $600,000 in chips and nobody else even had $60,000 when they started the final table. But that doesn't happen very often, so don't plan on it.

You cannot afford to lose your patience, I don't care what the situation is. The only way that you got this far (unless you were extremely lucky for a couple of days) is that you had enough patience to wait for hands in certain spots against certain people. I don't mean that you waited to pick up aces, kings, or queens. But you did wait for good hands and you got some play with them. That is, other people were in the pot with you when you got your good hands.

With A Short Stack

With a short stack you're just looking for a situation to get your money in. Suddenly two decent connectors start looking good to you—good connectors like K-Q, Q-J, J-10, 10-9, and ace-anything down to a nine (preferably suited). These are the types of hands you're looking for when you're playing short-handed with a small stack. You want to make sure that you see all five board cards.

The mistake a lot of players make in playing a short stack is putting part of their chips in when they should put *all* their chips in. They either just call or they make a small raise instead of raising with everything they have. Then they'll see a flop that doesn't hit their cards on the bulls-eye and they'll fold, whereas if they had been all-in, they might've made their hand on fourth or fifth street. The main point is that with a short stack, you have to make sure that you're going to see five cards.

The blinds are so high with only two tables in action, if you win the blinds two or three times, your short stack gets pretty close to being a medium stack. So there's nothing wrong with making some moves with a short stack. You know that someone's going to try to chop you off, so be at least a little selective on the hands you play. You can do it with the trouble hands, but you don't want to make a move with hands like 7-6 or 5-4 or K-6 or K-4. You know you're probably going to get called, so why not give yourself a pretty good chance of winning the pot? Wait for the types of hands I mentioned above—and of course, you could even pick up two aces. You know you're going to play your good hands, but you're also going to play the hands that spelled trouble earlier because they have become marginal hands that you have to play now that you're short-stacked at the second table.

You are not worried about your position at the table. You cannot control position when you're short-stacked. Ideally four people pass and you look down at A-9 with only one player behind you. That's beautiful—all of a sudden that A-9 looks like two aces! Your opponents are expecting you to play a hand when you will have to take the blind on the next deal. And they're expecting you to make a move with any two cards when you're on the button.

When You're Playing Against the Short Stack

Now suppose you're sitting directly to the left of the short stack and you have four players behind you. When he moves all in, are you going to make the loose call to try to knock him out in a situation where you can get chopped off from behind? You have to be very leery of what your position is in relation to the short stack and what his position is in relation to the rest of the field. You don't want him to drive you into total murder.

This is one reason why playing no-limit hold'em is so different from playing board games. In hold'em, position is everything. And your position to the short stack means so much. You know that the shortest stack on the table is going to have the blind on the next hand. Is he the type of player who's going to move in *now* with any face card from first position because he figures he might not get a face card in the blind? Do you think he's a good enough tournament player to know that if he wins the blinds, he will get another full round of the deal to pick up a hand? If he's that type of player, do you have enough of a hand to call him with, knowing that you could get rehashed from behind?

For example, suppose you know he will go all in with something like K-6 offsuit from first position. You're sitting in second position with A-5. You have four people sitting behind you. Are you willing to put your money in when you know that you can get chopped off from behind? That A-5 should go right into the muck. Let somebody else go after him. Throw away your trouble hands in this spot. Say that you're the second player behind him and you still have three players sitting behind you. But suppose you're the button with A-5.

In that case, you'll want to shut out the blinds so you'll probably reraise with the hand to try to play the short stack head-up. But if you don't really have a hand on the button and you reraise, you could be getting yourself into real trouble. You want to be careful that the short stack doesn't drive you into a big stack.

You have to be cognizant of every stack at the table, period—the short stacks, the medium stacks, and the big stacks. The short stacks can become large stacks very fast. I've seen it happen quite often. You cannot let the short stacks drive you into the big stacks. That's a cardinal sin.

Here's a scenario that illustrates what I'm talking about. Suppose the short stack goes all in from first position. You have a medium stack with a mediocre hand—a K-J or a small pair, for example—and four players are sitting behind you. How do you play your hand? You know that the blinds are coming to the short stack on the next deal, and he doesn't have to have much of a hand to play right now. But do you want to get yourself trapped in this hand? Suppose you call and somebody reraises you? You've just wasted the money you called with—you're not going to go for all your chips in this pot. And if you do, you're just looking for trouble.

Of course the people behind you might be good enough players to raise you on purpose. For example, I might not have a real reraise hand against you, but I might have a good enough hand to play the short stack and I can burn up your money in this spot and take you both out. That would be nice for me since I have plenty of chips and won't be hurting my stack with a reraise. You have to be leery of all these possibilities.

If the raiser is on your right, you always have to be cognizant of who is on your left, if you don't have a very good hand. Playing short-handed is not like playing head-up. When you're head-up, at least you know you're playing the man you're playing. But short-handed, you might start out playing one man and wind up playing another man. The short stack might not really figure into it because he probably doesn't have anything, but he has to play. You have something, but the guy to your right has more than you have. Now you're playing the guy who has more. The short stack you started out playing against can't really hurt you, but the second guy can destroy you. This is a trap you want to try to avoid so that you can get to the final table. All along the road to that final table, there are a lot of little, seemingly minor, trap doors that seem to spring open as you play, and you have to know where to step. You don't want to put yourself into situations where you can get killed before you get to where the real money is.

When you have people sitting behind you, you need to be wary of calling an all-in bet unless you have a hand that you can call a reraise with. Two different things can happen when you call with cards such as A-Q, A-J, or A-10:

1. You call and nobody raises;
2. You call and somebody raises behind you. You don't want to lose the opportunity to beat an all-in player, but you also don't want to lose a lot of chips. An A-Q, A-J, or A-10 might be good against the short stack, but these hands are not very good against a reraise. They can put you in a catch-22 situation.

Now if you're the last man to act and you have a mediocre hand and plenty of chips, you can call. There's a chance that you might have the best hand. When I say mediocre hand, I mean that you have a better than average hand, a K-Q, K-J, K-10 or a small ace or a small pair. Any of these hands might be the best hand against the all-in short stack. You know that the amount you call is the amount of money you're playing for—you're not playing for any extra money because he's all-in. You already know what kind of a chance you'll be taking with your hand.

Of course in this example, the only position from which you cannot get reraised is the big blind. Now say that a player has limped in from first position and the short stack, sitting to his left, comes over the top and goes all in. You're sitting on the button.

Remember that the limper is still alive in the pot and could beat you. You have to be leery of limpers at a short-handed table when the tournament is down to 12 or fewer players. You hardly ever see anybody limp at this point, so if a player limps in front of you, you have to be very, very careful about the hands you raise with because you could be reraised.

WHEN THE LAST TWO TABLES COMBINE

Let's suppose the two final five-handed tables have been combined into one table of 10 players. When it changes to 10-handed, you not only redraw for new seat assignments, you redraw for the button. Only nine players will make the official final table. You have the shortest stack and are about to bubble. What do you do?

When you're in tenth chip position with the short stack, that doesn't necessarily mean that you have a super short stack. You could be in one of those tournaments where everybody is fairly equal in chips. If that's the situation, then you just play a good, solid game of poker. Let the cards fall, and try to outlast people.

You don't want to bubble, of course, but still you're in a lot better circumstance than you were in when 11 players were left. Now you only have to post the big blind every 10 hands rather than once every five or six hands, unless you get very unlucky and draw the big blind when the tables combine. Depending on how many chips are in play, you can have the shortest stack on the table and still not be in really bad shape, but let's say that you are very short-stacked and you were unlucky enough to draw the big blind.

Big Blind is One-Half of Your Stack

By now the antes and blinds are big, so if you have more than a half of your stack in there for the big blind, and you'll have to put a half of your remaining chips in the small blind, you will just have to play the first hand you're dealt. If you get some action and are lucky enough to win the hand, you will have some chips. But if you wait until the small blind when you will have to put in a half of your remaining chips, even if you win the hand, you still won't have any more chips than you had in the first hand. This is why you have to make sure you play that first hand if more than half your money is already in the pot, no matter what your hand is or the action that is coming to you. With a short stack, you have to get lucky anyway, so play it. If you have 7-2, get lucky with it! It happens, you know.

Big Blind is One-Fourth of Your Stack

Now let's say that the big blind is one-fourth or less of your stack. In that case, you are not forced to play the hand. Don't rush. Wait. You have an entire round of the table to play and you might pick up a hand before you have to post the blinds again. When the big blind is one-fourth of your stack, the small blind is one-eighth of your stack. You will be putting in three-eights of your stack in the blinds, which means that you will have five-eights of your stack left in front of you. Then if you can double that up, you will have more chips than you started with. When you double up, you not only double up the blinds, you double up on the antes as well. When it's 10-handed in a big buy-in tournament, the antes are about $1,000 and the blinds are around $5,000-$10,000.

Suppose you have $24,000 in chips and you have to put up a $1,000 ante and a $10,000 big blind. In the next hand, you have to put in the $1,000 ante and the $5,000 small blind. Now you're talking about having to put up $16,000 out of your starting $24,000. In this case, you're forced to play your hand in the big blind.

But say that you have $44,000. You put up $11,000 and then $6,000, making $17,000 in antes and blinds, and leaving you with $27,000 in chips. If you just pick up the blinds in the next hand, you will get 10 times $1,000 (the antes) making $10,000, plus the $15,000 in blinds. You now have $25,000 plus the $27,000 you had left after posting the blinds for a total of $52,000, which is more than you started with. In this situation, you are not forced to play early on. That is, when you have at least four times the big blind plus the antes, the math tells you that you're not forced to play your hand in the big blind the first time around. Subtract $1,000 for each hand that is dealt until you come back to the big blind.

A lot of times when you get action, it will be from people who aren't in the blinds so that you can pick up not only the money you win in the hand, you pick up the blinds and the antes. When you win a pot, you get the $25,000 in blinds and antes, plus you double up your chips in the hand, and all of a sudden you've gone from $27,000 to $75,000 or $77,000. Now you're in good shape, you're back in the ballgame. And it doesn't take long. So use the mathematics to guide how you play, and don't get in a big hurry.

We already know that if you're real short-stacked, you have to play. If you lose the hand and get knocked out, so be it. You played the way you were supposed to play. But suppose you started with $22,000 and you win the pot. You win $5,000 from the little blind, you win all the antes, plus the money that was put into the pot that was equal to your all-in bet multiplied by the number of players in the pot against you. If you win that first pot you're forced to play, you will have enough chips to play for a while.

You have to be "tournament smart," and all these

factors have to register in your mind when you have a short stack. If you win two pots in a round, the money you win actually amounts to more than winning twice. Now you have chips. Now you can play your game, and let your opponents knock each other out. Every chip that you win, somebody else loses, which changes your ratio. And that ratio is going to continue to change, hopefully in your favor.

PART 6

Playing the Final Table

You have reached the final table with only nine players left in action. You've arrived among the cream of the crop. Now how can you rise to the top?

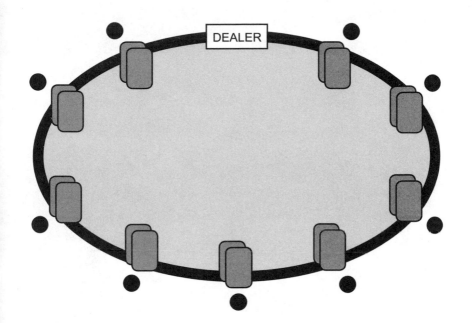

You've accomplished the hard part of the tournament, getting to the final table. Now you can relax and have some fun. Let the money you're playing for be in your thoughts, but keep it on the sideline. Play for the enjoyment of the game and you'll reap your reward as you get through it. Obviously, you have to think ahead and formulate a plan before you get there. You want to move up the ladder as far as you can, being careful as you're moving up it, yet still enjoy yourself.

A lot of players have fun trying to get to the final table, but once they get there, they stress out and freeze up. They're so scared they have a hard time moving their chips. They're worried about getting knocked out with this hand or losing a bunch of chips with that hand, so they don't really play their game. There's so much pressure there, and they don't know how to handle it. They're working while I'm playing!

I believe the pressure should be off your shoulders by the time you get there. I'm the most relaxed I can be when I'm at the final table. The tension is in getting there. Once you get there, you have to know how to play the final table, of course, but you don't need to make it into a stressful situation. Make it a fun situation. Enjoy yourself.

Keep your mind in the game. Don't let any outside distractions bother you. Nowadays with television and all the fans watching the final-table play, some players feel like they have to show off a little bit here and there, playing to the audience. And they make bad plays, sometimes just to be able to say, "I made the bluff, see what a great player I am?" Big deal! All you should be thinking about is, "How can I win that big pot of gold at the end of the rainbow?" With that thought planted in your mind, you only think about playing your best game. Anything that comes from TV or the fans will come to you when it's all over if you win it anyway, so why worry about it while you're playing the final table.

I've been a very competitive person all my life. I enjoy getting to a final table with every top player in the world because of the competitive nature of it. I like playing against the good players, and I'm relaxed when I'm playing them. I don't like losing at all! I don't say anything, but I take it very hard inside. At least, though, I really enjoy the competition. And I think everybody should. You put up your money for the opportunity to win some big money, so why not have a great time going for it?

WHEN YOU'RE PLAYING 10-HANDED

Although everyone goes to the final table when it gets down to 10-handed, the "official" final table doesn't begin until it's nine-handed. In 10-handed play, say that a lot of players have $60,000 and you have $50,000. The blinds are $3,000-$6,000 with a $1,000 ante. You're the shortest stack at the table, but you're not real short-stacked. You still have enough chips to play so you can wait for a good situation before you play a hand. Give yourself a chance to pick up some cards. Whether you pick up a hand on the first deal or on the fifth deal, so what? You've only lost $1,000 in each of the hands you passed, and at least you've given yourself a chance to pick up *that* hand. If you don't get dealt any playable cards, and your stack becomes real short, obviously you have to make a move. But first give yourself a chance to wake up with a hand by not rushing your play.

I usually formulate my plan in this way: I want this guy to knock that guy out, and go from there. Usually somebody has a commanding chip position. If he's an aggressive type of player, he'll do a lot of your work for you. Let him knock the other guys out. Let him work for you! The other guys will be raising hands and the chip leader will feel that since he has so many chips, he can play with them. Let him do it. Whether he wins or loses the pot, you gain something—either chip position in relation to him, or moving up a notch if he knocks somebody out. Every time he eliminates someone, you move up one spot and a lot of money on the pay scale. I always have the win in my mind, but I'm not a fool—I'm still going to try to get as much money out of the tournament as I can. And if I don't have to play a hand in the first round, and three or four guys get knocked out, I've probably picked up a couple hundred thousand dollars just by being patient.

Before the final table commences, I decide who I'm going to attack and who I'm not going to attack. I know who I'm going to be a little passive with. And I have it set in stone that I'm not going to play somebody's rush for them.

AT THE TELEVISION TABLE, THE "OFFICIAL" 9-HANDED FINAL TABLE

Finally we're down to the official final table of nine players, the televised table in World Series of Poker events. (In World Poker Tour tournaments, the televised table starts with six players.) If you're playing a World Series tournament, everybody has a lot of chips at the final table. You cannot compare a WSOP tournament with any other poker tournament except the WPT $25,000 buy-in championship event at the Bellagio because the amount of chips in play is so much larger in the World Series events than in any other tournaments because of the enormous size of the fields.

For example, 2,600-plus players entered the 2004 WSOP championship tournament. There were $26 million chips in play among the nine players at the final table! So, everybody had a lot of chips. And they weren't playing with blinds and antes so high that anybody was really short-stacked. The shortest stacks were down there around $100,000 or $200,000 when everybody else had millions. So, when we talk about big buy-in tournaments, we almost have to put the WSOP championship event into a separate category from the other $10,000 buy-in tournaments, simply because the other events usually have smaller fields and there aren't nearly as many chips in play at the championship table.

In most other big buy-in tournaments, the chips in play aren't nearly as large, so that when you get to the fourth day of those tournaments, the blinds are pretty high in comparison to the chips in play. Some tournaments are trying to take care of this disparity by adopting like-structures that are in line with the WSOP, but for quite a while, we were playing big tournaments where we had to play showdown hold'em when we hit the final table because the antes and blinds were so high. Now that most big buy-in tournament directors have adjusted their structures, you get some play at the final table. I attribute this change to television.

In World Poker Tour tournaments, the antes and blinds are actually lowered when the final table commences, going back a couple of levels, based on the number of entrants. They do this so that they will be able to shoot a couple of hours of television footage. Decreasing the antes and blinds at six-handed play actually works in the short-stacked players' favor because they have a better chance to play. (The rounds usually last for an hour, but when it gets to head-up play, they revert to half-hour levels.)

If you're at a final table where you know there's going to be a lot of play to it, play poker, *real* poker. Play the kind of poker you played to make it to the final table. You don't have to rush. But you do have to play every single player individually. One more time, let me say that when you hit that final table, you'd better find out how everybody is playing that day. Let me give you an example of how players can change their style of play at the final table. I watched Chris Karagulleyan on television as he played the final table of the Season One WPT Legends of Poker championship at the Bicycle Club. He played so, *so* tight when they were six-handed, but when they got down to three-handed, it seemed as though somebody else had taken over his seat. Chris opened his game up, playing almost any two cards, and won the whole enchilada.

That's not my style, but I mention it to illustrate how a player's style of play can change at any time. What I'm suggesting is that you should be able to recognize when it happens at the final table. If your opponents change their style of play, you have to change in accordance with how they are playing right *now*. If an opponent is playing super tight, obviously you can take a few pots away from him. But if he's playing super loose, you can't steal a pot from him any longer—he's going to call you.

One of the reasons why no-limit hold'em is such a terrific game is because of all the little nuances of the game you need to learn, and the things you need to be aware of. Your insights into the game, your instincts, and the knowledge that you carry with you through the years all come into play. A lot of guys have gotten there once and then you never hear from them again. For that one day, everything they did was right—whether it was good poker or bad poker, it worked for that day. But unless the exact same situations come up again, they never win again. What I'm trying to impart to you in this book is how to play well enough so that you can do it time and time again. Not that these strategies will work every time, but they will give you the best chance of winning.

Plan Your Play According to the Nature of Your Opponents

When the final table begins, I formulate my plan according to the players at the table, their seat position and chip position, my chip stack, and how many chips are in play. "Who can do what?" I ask myself. Is there a player here that I can absolutely run over, or are there players here that I can't run over, that I shouldn't try to run over because they're going to play? Is there a player at my table such as Erik Seidel? He has an innate sense of when to make the right call. He can call you down with a hand that most players wouldn't think about calling you down with—and be right. It doesn't work for him every time, of course, but he is top notch at it.

Are there aggressive players at my table such as Layne Flack, Paul Phillips, Freddy Deeb or Antonio Esfandiari? These are guys who love to play a lot of hands. How are you going to play them? Say you have Paul Phillips here and you have Mel Judah, a solid player, over there. Mel is usually going to have a real hand when he comes into a pot. He isn't going to try to play as many pots as Paul does. Are you going to play Mel and Paul the same way?

At the final table, I'll play more pots than I did earlier because I'm going to try to attack this guy or that guy in certain situations. But I won't play as many pots as players like Paul, who raise a lot of pots whether or not they have a hand. Daniel Negreanu also is a very aggressive player. And I'm going to play him and the other aggressive players differently than I play someone like Mel or Chip Reese or Doyle Brunson. Doyle can surprise the hell out of you, though—he'll play solid for a long time and then all of a sudden, he'll raise with something like 10-2. Mel, Chip, Doyle and I play along the same lines. We all do these kinds of things, but we don't make a habit of doing them. If you're going to try to steal a pot, you try to take it from a *player*. You don't try to steal it from a loose player who got there by being lucky, because you know that he's going to call you with any two cards.

If I had to play Gus Hansen at the final table, I would play him completely differently than anybody else I've mentioned, including Daniel and Paul. Gus will put his money in there if he figures he has one live card that he can beat you with. You've got to know these things about players. Gus has been very successful with his style of play, and if he can adjust his game here and there, he has enough card sense to be capable of lasting over a long period of time.

Then there's Howard Lederer, who they call "the professor." He has his nights, too, and has done fantastically well on the tournament circuit. He and Erik Seidel have always been great players and are now playing more tournaments than they used to play.

They both play a little more along my style of play, but each of us has a certain personal skill that is different from the others. Mine is observation, being a pretty good reader of my opponents, and seizing situations that come my way. Erik can make the long call better than anybody. Howard is deliberate and moves his game around enough to keep people on their guard. He goes through the same routine on every hand, cutting out his chips in a particular way, so that you can't pick up a tell on what he's playing. I've seen him do it with a 6-4 and I've seen him do it with two aces, so he leaves you dangling out there trying to figure out what he has in the hole.

All top players have certain skills that are their own, and when you're playing at a final table, you need to know what they are. If you have any poker smarts at all, you can pick up on what's going on. With me, it may be a little easier because I have all these years of experience behind me. I may be just a touch older than most players on the tournament circuit, but I haven't forgotten a damn thing.

The best advice I can give you when you're playing a final table is this: learn something about a player on every single hand. When a hand goes to the showdown, you're going to see the cards the opponents played. Remember how they played their cards in that situation, and learn something. Hell, I learn things all the time.

Remember that most tournaments end for the day when it gets to the final table. So, when you return the next day and start anew, you need to find out how your opponents are playing after taking the evening off. You probably already know what their patterns are, and you know that at some point, they're going to fall into their patterns. Now take your analysis to the next level and ask yourself, "How are they playing *today*?" Are they adding to their usual pattern today? Or are they taking something away from their pattern today? I've seen people who played super poker to get to the last table, but after they got there, they actually played horrible. When I say horrible, I mean raising with something like 9-3 on the button and then calling a reraise.

Play Your Best Game

Getting to the final table doesn't matter if you don't finish it off by playing your best game. You cannot get there and then say to yourself, "I'm satisfied," because if you think that way, you may let your guard down. The final hand you lose may be a bad beat, but you probably wouldn't have been in that situation if you hadn't played some other hands poorly before that. These things can happen if you become too complacent and let your guard down.

If the cards are shuffled right now, and a millisecond later they're shuffled again, you know that different hands are going to be dealt. If you hadn't played that 9-3 when you did, it would've been a different time zone, and something would've been different so that you probably would not have been dealt the hand that you got broke to at the end. So, everything that you do now affects what happens later. That's just the way life is, and it's especially true in poker.

Every time the cards are shuffled, something different is going to happen. The point is that what you do all the way through the play at the final table usually leads up to your end result. If you hadn't played bad and attempted something you shouldn't have in Hand 8, then Hand 30 wouldn't have been there for you to go broke on. Hand 30 would've been a different hand, and who knows what the result might have been? Your actions in the present moment greatly affect your results in the future. This all sounds ethereal, I know, but things happen that way in life and in poker.

One year at the Bicycle Club, I was playing in a no-limit hold'em side game with Al Krux. Al went all in for his case money with pocket kings and I called him on the button with pocket tens. But the dealer didn't see that I had called, so she dropped the deck on the muck. The floorman ruled that she had to reshuffle all the cards in the muck and then deal the flop. The flop came K-10-4-10-3. I put such a bad beat on Al it was pitiful! But if the dealer hadn't dropped the deck on the discard pile, those two tens that had been discarded would never have been in play for me to make quad tens and send Al to the rail, would they? It's something like the concept in physics that for every action there is an opposite action. These things happen in poker, too.

You can control what happens to you, but you cannot control a lot of other things. For example, the only time that I feel I ever played perfect poker was at the 2000 WSOP final table when Chris Ferguson and I got heads up. But something was in the mix that led up to the final hand. Chris told me that he didn't think he could beat me that day. I'm not saying that he thought he couldn't beat me some other day, but the way I was playing, he didn't think he could beat me *that* particular day. So, he concluded that he had to take a chance on a hand. Well, he just happened to take a chance on the right hand when he played an A-9 against my A-Q. All the way through the hand, it looked as though he had blown the championship. But when that nine hit on the river, it didn't look that way at all! His timing was perfect. Chris is a great poker player—and he has a terrific mind to go with it all.

I look at poker somewhat as though people are playing chess. Chess players think about three or four moves ahead, and that's what I do when I'm playing at a final table. I'm always thinking about what's going to happen down the road. I act fast on all my hands because I know in advance what I'm going to do if such and such comes off the deck, if certain cards come on the board. Tom is getting into the flow, feeling real good about his play, and is taking things easy right now. Mark is starting to get a little itchy, and I figure he's going to start making some moves.

So, who am I going to play? The guy who's getting edgy, not the one who's feeling confident. I may not be in the hand when I notice these things, but I'm going to be in some hand in the near future. I want to be in pots with the guy who's starting to get upset, or the one who has just lost a big pot. Maybe these kinds of observations are what set you apart—maybe that's why you win and they don't. Thinking ahead is good. It should be a part of your plan for the day.

Play Carefully When You Have a Medium Stack

When it gets to nine players, you have to think about your goals. Your final goal is to win it, but how are you going to accomplish that? How are you going to go about playing? Now that you're down to where the money counts, every place you move up usually is significant in money. So, you notice who has the big stacks and who has the short stacks, and compare how you stand with them in the chip count.

Say that you have an average stack and a couple of guys have shorter stacks than you do. You not only want to win the tournament, you also want to make sure that you do as well as you can along the way. Typically the player who has the big lead is the one who takes out the short stacks. He's usually the player who has been holding the most hands and if the short stacks get short enough, the big lead will call with a very marginal hand to try to take them out. You want the short stacks to get knocked out before you start opening up your game so that you're moving up the scale at all times. This should always be in the back of your mind.

Suppose you have $200,000 and the short stacks have $50,000 on average. You're in pretty good shape. There may be players with a lot more chips than you have, but still you're in good shape versus the short stacks. You don't want to be putting in your chips with marginal hands because, since the antes and blinds are so high, the short stacks are going to be forced to play. Give them a chance to go out. If one of them doubles up, somebody else's stack is going to be depleted— and you don't want it to be your stack.

My strategy in this situation is not to be overly aggressive. You want to play your good hands, but you don't want to be too aggressive and allow yourself to get knocked out early. You don't want to make mistakes. Naturally you don't want to ever make any mistakes in a poker tournament, but you definitely don't want to make any mistakes at the final table. So, give the short stacks a chance to knock themselves out. If they double up, let them double through somebody else. When you play a hand, have a real hand. You'll find that you can move up the ladder with this strategy when you have an average stack. And when you have a big-big stack, play it the same way I've suggested playing an average stack.

When you have a small stack, you're looking to play a hand. Your criteria for the kinds of hand you can play have to be set by the amount of chips you have. If you're real short, just find something you like and go with it. Hopefully, you'll double up if someone plays with you and you win the hand. Then you're back in the ballgame.

But the medium stack is the one you really have to play carefully. If nothing else, when a few players at the table have less chips than you have, you want to make sure that you make it to a higher place than they do. Money-wise, it makes quite a bit of difference as you climb the pay scale. But you always try to do it with the "I'm gonna win this tournament" attitude. You have to get to one point before you can get to the next point. If you just hold your share of the cards, you're going to increase your chips here and there, so long as you don't take any bad beats.

Bad beats are just a part of poker, and there's nothing you can do about them. My main advice is that if you take a beat, bad or otherwise, do not let it affect your play for the rest of the tournament. Say that you had $200,000 and you lose $50,000 in a hand, leaving you with $150,000 in chips. You still have enough chips to play with so don't let the beat affect your play. Don't sizzle. Players these days are good enough that they will test you after you lose a pot to see whether you're sizzling or getting out of line. Just play your game; you'll find that it works. It does for me. I just stay away from going crazy after I lose a hand or take a beat. I may be feeling it inside but I'm not going to show it on my face and I'm not going to show it in my play. Look at the glass as being half full rather than half empty.

Always Maintain a Positive Attitude

No matter what bad things happen to your good hands, you still want to play your best poker. That means coming in with decent hands, playing the quality of hands you played at the start of the tournament. You're playing at a full table again, not at a short table like you were just before the final table began. And even though the antes and blinds are higher now, if you have an average to large stack, your stack is higher too. It's all relative.

Don't make the mistake of thinking that you have to pick up the blinds all the time. Suppose you're not successful in doing that. Maybe you're on the button, it's passed to you, and you raise with a bad hand. The blind calls and you lose the pot. That loss can put you in a bad frame of mind. "Why did I do that?" you wonder. "That was stupid. Why should I try to win x-amount of money and sacrifice more than what I could win to do it?" If you're in a bad or negative mood, you're more likely to make another mistake. The idea is not to make the first mistake. Let the other guys make the mistakes.

It's so hard not to make mistakes playing hold'em. You want to be aggressive, and you want to take this pot and take that pot. And there are times to do it. But when you're playing nine-handed at the final table is not the time to do it. You're playing at a full table, just like you were at the start of the tournament. Remember this important fact: The more hands dealt out, the bigger hand it takes to win a pot. When 18 cards are coming off the deck versus only 10 cards coming off it, more cards are out to make more big hands possible. That's why, when we used to play 11-handed in Dallas in the old days, it took a helluva hand to win a pot because there were a lot cards in play. After you get to short-handed play, and especially when you get to head-up play, you can understand why certain hands have a lot more value than they do when you're playing nine-handed. But at the start of the championship table, you're playing in a full ring game. You're no longer playing short-handed like you were at two tables, when the hand values were different. So you have to readjust your play when you start out at the final table.

PLAYING SEVEN-HANDED

Now let's assume that we've lost the short stacks and are down to seven players. You started with an average stack, you've moved up several spots on the ladder, and have made some extra money. You know that if something bad happens, you at least have seventh place locked up. You still have winning as your goal, but how are you going to attain it?

After all is said and done, you have to catch some cards. And hopefully, you will catch them in the right situation so that you will make some money on them. The most dismal thing that can happen is that you finally pick up pocket aces or kings, and everybody passes. At least, you didn't lose anything with them, but you didn't get the action you wanted.

You're in your mode, you've played a while, you're into the flow of the game. You know who's doing what, how they're playing, what they're capable of doing. You have noticed who has become overly aggressive, playing too many pots. You realize that a guy can have a rush of cards, but maybe not so big a rush that he can raise three of five pots. When an opponent does that, you know he's being overly aggressive, so you start looking for a spot where you can do something to him. His criteria for the hands he plays have dropped. You know that because he's making all these moves. He may be in too big a hurry to win the tournament. Many times it seems that the player in the chip lead or the one who has the second-biggest stack are the ones who get overly aggressive. They've gotten a hold of all those chips, and now they think that they can bully the table. Plus, it's probably a new day, and what worked yesterday might not work today. This is why you sometimes see one of the chip leaders go out early.

You're trying to play your best poker, all the while seizing every situation you can. Once in a while, you have to make a little move at the pot. But seven-handed, I believe that I'm still at the stage where it isn't wise to move all in when I raise. If I move in, it's because somebody has already raised and I believe that I have the best hand. Then I'm going over the top of them with a move-in bet trying to get them to double me up. I'm still playing good cards. Usually there are three or four players at the final table who are inexperienced in tournament play. When they raise, they're usually going to raise their whole stack, and you've got to like that. But if you call, you must believe that you have the best hand, not a marginal hand.

Having three or more people who are inexperienced tournament players at the final table is a new wrinkle in today's tournament milieu. When they raise they often raise all in, instead of playing out the pot. You have to adjust to them. The inexperienced players just want to get it all in and then play showdown poker because they can't get outplayed that way. The experienced player wants to play the pot out because whether he has the best of it or not, he can use his tournament skills to beat less experienced players in the play of the hand. A lot of times, too, there will be someone who is well known at the final table and their intimidation factor is strong, really strong. People ask themselves, "How am I gonna beat this guy? He's won a ton of titles." And they really mean it. It's always in the back of their minds, so they're sort of whipped to start with

When you're playing seven-handed, you're not really shorthanded but you're not in a full ring game either. You still need to maintain high standards of play. In other words, you have to play solid poker. You're not playing a pot with baby pairs unless it's small blind against big blind heads-up, or the button against the two blinds. Even then, you're not moving in with them. You're not playing hands like K-Q or Q-J up front, because if you get played with and you flop one of your rank, you're in kicker trouble.

Suppose you have K-Q and the flop comes Q-3-2. If you get action on the hand, you're usually in very bad trouble, so you try to stay clear of those traps. It looks like you have a huge hand, but if you're up against an A-Q, you're got a piece of toilet paper. Or what if the flop comes A-Q-2? Now what are you going to do with your K-Q? If it's checked to you on the flop and then off comes a blank, are you going to bet it on fourth street? What if your opponent was slow-playing an ace?

You don't want to play a hand that can get you into trouble on the flop or even on fourth street. You want to play hands with which you are in the controlling position. I'm not saying that you can't play K-Q or K-J or something like that from the button or from one of the blinds when nobody has come into the pot. If you have noticed that people are coming into pots with hands like J-10 or Q-J or Q-10, for example, and you pick up one of those hands from around back, go ahead and play it if you want. Just remember that any drunk can wander in off the street and pick up a big hand in a poker game. He's going to get the same number of good hands as you do in the long run.

Further, you are not standing raises with hands like A-10, even though someone else might be raising with A-J, A-10 or A-9. I'm not saying that you shouldn't try to pick up the pot with this type of hand when you're sitting around back, but you're definitely not calling with it. You might raise with it, but you can't call a raise with it.

Of course, any hand with an ace in it becomes stronger and stronger as you move up the ladder. An ace is always a powerful card. Even if someone has two kings and you have an A-2, you might catch an ace on the board and beat him. Of course, you prefer having two overcards to your opponent's pair. Remember that if an opponent has a pocket pair and you have two overcards to it, you're only an 11 to 10 dog. A lot of tournaments get down to who wins the "race," the coin-flip hands such as A-K against pocket jacks. But even with A-K, you are still an underdog in this situation. More tournaments are won or lost with A-K than any other hand I can think of. The idea is for your opponent to always be the underdog with you as the favorite.

In summary, when you're seven-handed, you still want to have a hand before you put your money in the pot. You're into decent money, but you're not into real money yet. Real money starts at third place on up. You're still not playing short-handed so your standards for the hands you play still have to be high. You're playing solid poker.

PART 7

Six-Handed at the Final Table

The short stacks are standing on the rail. You need to outlast only five more opponents to reach your ultimate goal of winning the tournament.

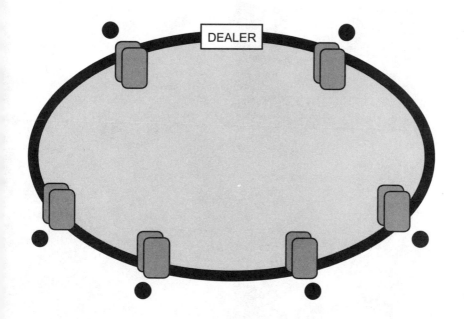

When you make it to the final six in a World Poker Tour tournament, the action stops for the day, your chips are placed in plastic bags and stored in the vault, and you return to your hotel room to get some rest. While you're sleeping, the TV crew puts the set in place, gets the cameras ready to roll, and sets up the bleachers for the television live audience. The next day you will make your appearance on the world stage of tournament poker, with Mike Sexton and Vince Van Patten scrutinizing your every play. And that's when the fun begins.

When you're at six players, keep in mind that the real money is in the top three spots. You want to get to that top three before you start taking a lot of chances. If you have sized up the opposition correctly, you know who to play against and what kinds of hands you can successfully play against them. Be selective about the hands you play, be careful about your position at the table when you play them, take your chip count into consideration, and play every opponent differently. Most importantly, combine all these factors into a plan for winning the tournament. Your plan will give you added confidence when the TV cameras start to roll and the pressure is on.

START OFF WITH A PLAN

Your chip count, the nature of your opponents, and your position at the table are three of the most important considerations in planning your play at the final table six-handed. Your opponents might have you out-chipped by 2 to 1, but if you know in your heart that you're a 3 to 1 better player than they are, play your game. Be honest with yourself when you're making these types of evaluations: you know whether you can play, and you know what they can do.

Your chip count probably is the biggest factor in planning your strategy. If you're the short stack, you can't let your stack just dwindle away. You have to get a hold of all the chips to win the tournament, so at some point you have to give yourself a chance to get some chips rather than just trying to stay alive. Staying alive is okay if you want to move up a place or two, which is always nice. But then you're throwing in the towel as to winning the tournament. And of course I always have my sights on winning. I want to get to third or second place because the money's good there, and if I get knocked out at least I'll have a nice payday. But I never forget that my ultimate goal is the win.

Putting A Plan Into Action at the 2000 WSOP

Winning was my goal in the 2000 WSOP championship event, even though I started with the smallest stack. My plan was to let the other players knock themselves out playing against each other, and I knew that Chris Ferguson, the overwhelming chip leader, was going to go to work to knock them out. I decided in advance not to play unless I had a premium hand, and to make positional plays with decent hands when they came up in spots where I could steal the pot. We were six-handed at the start and I didn't want to get into any big confrontations until we got short-handed. My goal was to get head-up with Chris.

Luckily I had a lot of final-table experience, but most of my opponents didn't, so I figured they would be in a hurry to get a hold of some chips. A couple of players went out right off the bat, going all-in with an A-Q against an A-4, or something similar. The only time I made a play was against Hasan Habib when it was passed to him on the button and I was in the big blind. When he raised the pot, I knew that he was capable of raising with a very marginal hand to try to steal the blinds. All I had was K-10, but I thought that, at the worst, I had two overcards, and might be able to win the hand with a bet. It was time for me to start gathering a few chips. I reraised him and Hasan beat me into the pot with pocket deuces. We got it all in, I made two pair to beat him, and doubled up. That was a key hand for me.

When Chris and I got head-up, I was very selective in the hands that I played, so that every time I played a pot, I either had the best hand or got the best flop. My idea was to get full value out of every hand I played and chip away at Chris's stack. You see, even though your opponent may have a lot more chips than you, you want to put him on the defensive, get him to start worrying. "Hey, my lead is shrinking," you want him to start thinking. "This guy's outplaying me and I've gotta do something to get back on track."

Using this plan, I actually took the lead at one point. The plan worked, it just didn't carry me all the way through. You're going to find that some times, your plan in hold'em tournaments will work up to a certain point—but you still have to contend with the luck factor. On the final hand, my A-Q against his A-9, he caught a nine to beat me on the river. You can overcome most of the luck factor by continually giving yourself a chance to win by getting your money in with the best hand. If somebody draws out on you, at least you can go to bed at night and say, "I played as well as I could play."

SIZE UP YOUR OPPONENTS

When you get to the final table, size up your opponents, know their capabilities, and determine how they are playing that day. You usually know how they play most of the time, but how are they playing today? Everybody reverts to form sooner or later, but they may not start out that way; it may take them a while to get into their pattern. Play your opponents according to what you predict they're going to do, or what they're doing right then. Use what they're doing to fortify your play against them. Play your strengths against their weaknesses.

If you know that an opponent will play any two paints, use that against him. Or maybe you know that when he comes in, he only comes in with premium big cards, or a big pair, or at least a pair. So you say to yourself, "When I play a hand against him, I'm gonna have a good holding over the type of holding he usually plays." So if he's the type of guy that will play K-Q, K-J, K-10, Q-J, or Q-10, you should at least have an ace and a big card in your hand when you play against him. An ace with a big card is good anytime, and in shorthanded play, an A-10 also picks up value. If you figure he's playing something like a K-10 and you have an A-10, imagine what an edge you have over him.

Another opponent at your table might be a player that will risk his chips with something like a 9-8 suited. You see that so often at the final table in televised events. You want to keep your requirements better than that. So if you have something like an A-J or A-Q against this type of player, you can play with him because you know he has a tendency to play the middle suited connectors. You also know that somebody else might be able to take him off, so don't force things. You don't have to be the player who eliminates everybody. Your main goal is to eliminate only one player—the last player.

Playing Against Super-Aggressive Opponents

Judging from what we see on TV, today's mode of play at the final table is very aggressive. Some players have trouble modifying their playing style to defend against their super-aggressive opponents. Here is an idea of how you might adjust to playing against an aggressive player, Paul Phillips in this example. At the Bicycle tournament Paul and I were playing at the final table in three-handed action. All day long I made the same size raise, he would come over the top of me, and a lot of times I would throw my hand away.

The whole day I kept track of the amount that I raised. Finally I looked down at two jacks. I had been setting up this play for a couple of hours, and made sure that I put in the exact same raise I had been making all day long. And here he came, all-in. This time I beat him into the pot. Unfortunately, he had pocket sevens, flopped a seven, and won the pot. But the point is that I got the play I wanted, and the reason I got it was because I kept doing exactly the same thing in order to entice the play.

Later I watched the Bike tournament on TV, and saw several of the hands I played with Paul. At the time I knew he didn't have a hand every time he raised, and some of those times, I didn't have a hand either;

I was just making a little play at the pot. But I always made sure to make the same raise. I had enough chips and I was hopeful that the time would arrive when he would come over the top and I would be able to just zoom right in on him.

Top players do this—they set up plays at the final table. Of course there are other ways to set up plays according to the nature of your opponents. Suppose a solid player is at the final table. Six or five-handed you have noticed that he plays a K-Q very strong. Knowing this, you can make a little raise with an ace-something and, hopefully, he will come back at you.

Sometimes your opponents set themselves up by getting overly aggressive on hands. You know it's coming, so you're hopeful that you catch a hand (not necessarily a big hand, just a good hand) in a situation where you can take that money away from them. Sometimes I do it with nothing. If I see a guy raising too often in front of me, I just go over the top of him. Hopefully, of course, it's at a time when he doesn't have a hand.

When I pick up chips, I want to pick up more than just the antes. A lot of people are satisfied with stealing antes, but that's not my forte. If I'm going to steal a pot, I want to have some of their money plus the antes in there. I don't do it that often, so they have to figure out when I have a hand and when I don't have a hand. I put the decision to them.

Putting a Power Play on a Short Stack

At the final table you can put a power play on one of the short stacks when you know that he's trying to hang on, or when he has enough chips to move up the ladder if he can win a hand while the other short stacks are trying to hang on and improve their positions on the pay scale.

Suppose just you and one of the short stacks are in a hand. He has come into the pot and you've put him on a mediocre hand such as pocket eights or sevens. You know he just wants to hang on for as long as he can. You think that he will lay his hand down against a raise. It's not so much what your hand is, it's how much money he has in his stack, and how much of that money is in the pot that determines whether you put in a power raise against him

For example, suppose he has $40,000 and has made it $8,000 to go. You have a ton of chips and come over the top of him to put him all in. You're not raising on the strength of your cards, you're raising on the weakness of his chip position. You're putting him to the test. He has a big decision to make: "Is my hand good enough that I am willing to go out of the tournament with it?"

However if he only has $16,000 left in his stack and he bets $8,000, you can't make this move against him because he is already pot-committed and will call any raise. That is, any time the short stack has one-half his chips already in the pot, you must have a hand to make a power raise because you know that the short stack will be forced to call your raise.

SELECT THE HANDS YOU PLAY CAREFULLY

Say we're down to six-handed and I get a hand like A-J. I might raise with this hand, but I probably won't call a raise with it. There's a big difference in raising with this type of hand, and calling a raise with it. If somebody raises in front of me, they're telling me, "I think I have a good enough hand to raise this pot." Then I ask myself, "Is A-J a good enough hand to call them with?" I know it's a good enough hand to raise with, especially from around back, but is it strong enough to call with?

When I say A-J or better, I'm not talking about pocket deuces or sixes (or any of the low pairs) although I know they're better hands. Heads up, they're 11 to 10 favorites, but they're not a big favorite when you're playing six or seven-handed against the whole field because any overcard that comes on the board can make them look silly. I don't play those small and middle pairs unless we're very short-handed.

You see people move in all their chips with small to medium pairs whenever they're the first one in the pot. I don't like that play at all. Other players are sitting behind you and they could have a better starting hand than you. Realize that if you have pocket sixes and somebody with 8-7 plays with you, you're only an 11-to-10 favorite. With that in your mind, you don't just move all in all the time.

A factor that a lot of players don't think about is this: when you have a baby pair and you're up against two overcards, the board can double-pair with cards that are higher than your baby pair. And then your opponent's high card works as a kicker and you're a goner. This happens a lot more times than you might think. You've got pocket threes and the board comes 5-5-4-8-8. Your opponent has a 10-9. His kicker is a 10; your kicker is a three. I've been right lots of times in my career when I've made a long call in these situations with the best kicker on a double-paired board.

Now let's say the board comes K-7-7 and I have pocket sixes. My opponent raised before the flop and now he makes a bet at the pot on the flop. I call him because I believe I have the best hand, and I think that all he has is two overcards to the pair. Then the board double-pairs with another king—at the river it's K-7-7-K-9. I was right when I got my money in, but his kicker beat me on the end. It's the sickest feeling in the world to make that long call and be right, and then see the board double-pair to negate your pair. You know you made the right play when you called on the flop, but Lady Luck just ate you alive.

Inexperienced final-table players sometimes get nervous when they make it to the final table, worrying about how they should play. Some novices try to compensate for their lack of experience by moving in on every hand they play. They don't want to see a lot of flops because they're afraid of getting outplayed by the pros. If you decide to move in, you should have the nuts. But why not play the hand out so that you can get full value from it? Most of the time when you move in, all you get is the money that is in the pot at the moment. And if you move in and get called, you might not have the best hand.

If you are new to final-table play, I advise you to get your act together as soon as possible. Keep your eyes on the prize and don't let anyone or anything distract you. Play in accordance with how your opponents are playing. Don't ever be afraid to play a pot out. If you play a pot out, there are a lot of situations where you can outplay a man to win the pot. At other times, move in. Do whatever the situation calls for. You don't want to give yourself a chance to get out-played by freezing up. The good players can sense when you have just a little bit of weakness and they will try to take advantage of that.

PLAY IN POSITION

Hold'em is a game of position. When you play a hand, you want to have position over your opponents so that they have to act first. When they have to act first on each street, you have a big edge. Their checks and the amount of their bets give you a lot of information. You want to be the receiver of information, not the giver. If you raise from early position with a marginal raising hand and an opponent calls you, you'll have to act first after the flop, so you don't raise the pot. In fact you might not even play the pot because you will be out of position after the flop. The whole idea is to make your opponent act first unless you have a big enough hand to be able to set him up, in which case you hope he catches something on the flop because you have the boss hand.

You've probably heard that you shouldn't let any free cards come off in tournaments. I don't entirely agree with that. Say that the flop comes with two clubs and you have two aces or even a set, and a guy plays with you. Most people would never check their hand, but I might check to get a play later in the hand. Just because my opponent plays with me, I don't necessarily put him on a flush draw. If another flush card comes and he gets very active when it comes off, maybe he did have a flush draw after all. Then you have to make a decision. But just because two of a suit are showing on the board when you're against only one opponent doesn't mean that he has that suit. And just because you *don't* have that suit doesn't mean that he does have it. Don't be overly afraid of these types of scary flops.

Don't be an idiot either. Suppose you raise the pot with A-K or A-Q and get called. If the flop comes with any paint or a 10, you might be up against a better hand. Or suppose you made a little raise before the flop and your opponent called. Now the flop comes with three to a straight—10-9-8. Nothing says that he might not have a J-10 or two jacks in his hand.

The sets are obvious, but these types of flops are not as obvious. A straight draw, or a pair with a straight draw, could be out. People are going to play those types of hands. You have to be leery of what the board is showing, but you don't necessarily have to put your opponent on the best hand every single time. And that is why you play out a pot rather than making a big move.

Or suppose you raised before the flop with K-K, someone called, and the flop comes with J-10-9. Your opponent checks to you and you move in. If he calls your bet, he probably has K-Q or a set. So why move in when he checks to you? Why not just make a decent bet instead? If you win the pot, fine. If your opponent calls you, fine. If he raises, then you can make your decision. You've only put a certain amount of chips in the pot rather than putting your whole tournament in jeopardy.

People have a habit of putting their entire tournament in jeopardy by moving in every time they play a pot. If they're wrong when they move in, they're gone. Say that you have $100,000 in front of you and you bet $5,000. Somebody comes over the top of you and you decide to lay it down. You still have $95,000 to play with. Now suppose you're in a hand with two opponents, and you bet $100,000 on the flop.

One opponent moves in and the next one comes into the pot after him. Your chances of winning this pot probably are slim and none. So why not just make a regular bet at the pot on the flop instead of going all in? That way, your opponents will tell you where you stand in the hand, and you can then decide your best play.

Sometimes you can send a boy to do a man's job. When you can send a certain amount of chips out there to do the job, why send your whole stack? That certain amount probably will win the pot for you anyway, and if your opponent has a big hand, at least you haven't blown your whole stack. It's a way of cutting your losses if you don't have the best hand, and giving yourself a better chance of at least staying in the tournament.

KNOW HOW TO PLAY YOUR RELATIVE POSITION IN THE CHIP COUNT

Your chip count relative to your five opponents strongly influences your strategy at the final table. At the 2000 WSOP championship event, I knew that every six hands I'd have to put in the $20,000 blind, but I also realized that I had enough time to let my opponents destroy themselves in pots. If a hand came out against another hand, someone was going to lose—and I was going to move up the ladder. And in the WSOP when you move up the ladder, you really move up in the money. In fact once you get to six players at the final table in any of the big $10,000 events like the WSOP and the WPT, you're talking about winning another $100,000 or more every time you move up one rung on the ladder. And when it's down to the last three players, the jumps are a lot more than that. And that's enough money to be willing to be patient enough to give yourself a chance to win it.

Now, here are some tips on how to play your chip position with a short stack, medium stack, and a big stack.

When You Have a Small Stack

A lot of players who start the final table with the shortest stack say to themselves, "Oh-my-gawd, this guy's got a million and that guy's got three million and I've only got $100,000. I've gotta play right now!" But I'm here to tell you that you don't have to. If the blinds are fairly low, you don't have to play the very first hand. Obviously you want to play when you get a decent hand, but you don't have to play any marginal hands that aren't really playable.

There are two things to think about when you have a short stack. One, you know that eventually you will have to take a stand. Two, you want to try to survive long enough to get to the top three. If you have the shortest stack at the final table, it matters how short your stack is. At the 2000 WSOP championship table, I had the shortest stack but I wasn't in dire straits yet. The blinds were $5,000-$10,000 with a $1,000 ante, and I had $216,000. If I caught a hand and doubled up, I'd still have plenty of chips. I didn't need to search for a hand to play right away. So, if you have the shortest stack and you're not in imminent danger, play your game, be patient.

Now let's say that I had $50,000 in chips rather than over $200,000, and the rest of the field had $400,000 with one player over $2 million in chips. In that case, I would have been looking for any two good cards to play because the blinds would eat me up anyway. By any two good cards, I mean any ace, any king with a decent kicker, or any pocket pair. For example, when I got to the final table in the WPT championship event in Reno, I was the short stack by a long shot and knew that I had to play the first decent hand I was dealt. When I got pocket sevens, I moved in. Unfortunately, I ran into two aces.

When you're extremely short-stacked, you never want to get yourself into the situation where even if you double up, it won't matter much. Say you only have $50,000 and the blinds are $5,000-$10,000 with an ante of $500. Playing six-handed, it's costing you $18,000 per round to play. You need to play a hand pretty quickly and try to double up while you still have your $50,000. If you go through the blinds one time, you will have $32,000 left in your stack. (Remember you're still anteing every hand.) Let's say that by the time you play a hand, you have $30,000. If you double up when you have $30,000, you'll have $60,000, and you aren't much better off than when you started out. The point is that you want to take a chance to double up when it will really mean something, when $50,000 will turn into $100,000. Or maybe you'll be able to triple up against two opponents and build your stack to $150,000. Then you can play the game.

In other words, you can't afford to let yourself get so short-stacked that even if you double up, you'll be right back where you started. It doesn't matter which two cards you play. I remember a situation in which I had only $18,000 with the blinds at $3,000-$6,000 and a $500 ante. I was in the big blind for $6,000. It was passed to Paul Ladanyi on the button, and he raised enough to move me all in. I looked down at a 7-2, the worst hand you can get in hold'em.

"The next hand, I'll have to put up $3,000 plus the $500 ante," I thought to myself, "and then I'll be way down in chips." My reasoning was that, if he didn't have a pair—if he was playing an ace-something—I was only a 2 to 1 underdog. Two overcards with five cards to come is only a 2 to 1 favorite against two random cards. I had $6,500 in the pot and I'd have to put in $3,500 in the next hand, leaving me with less than half of my stack after paying the two blinds. Considering my chip position, I had to make a move right then. If I lost the $6,000 I had in the pot, I'd be right back where I started, even if I won the next hand. I beat him into the pot with that 7-2! He had an A-J and I flopped a deuce to win the pot. That double-up win carried me onward to winning second place in the tournament.

Situations like this where you must make your move with any two cards come up at the final table all the time. You just hope that you're right when you do it, that your opponent doesn't have a pocket pair. I would want both of my hole cards to be "live," so I would prefer playing them against an A-x or a K-x. When I say live, I mean that the two cards he has in his hand do not duplicate my two hole cards. (And believe me, with a 7-2, there's a pretty good chance your cards are not duplicated!) Then if I flop a pair and he doesn't flop a pair, I will be in the lead. Obviously if neither of us flops a pair, the high card will win.

If six experienced players are at the final table—people you know, players with names in poker—they aren't going to give you a chance to wait them out. They're going to be waiting it out themselves; they know how important it is to get to the top three. In that case, you have to use a different strategy: You have to open up and play a little bit. But if four of your opponents are basically new to playing a final table, and the chip leader is someone you know is aggressive enough to try to knock each one of them off, then you use the type of strategy I used in 2000. Let them knock each other out.

Since most of them don't have much experience, the chances are good that they're going to play any decent ace for a lot of money instead of just taking a flop to it and seeing the board cards before they get all their money in.

There's a lot to be said for just taking a flop sometimes. But there's also the reverse side to that: by just calling, you're taking a risk when you let your opponents see a cheap flop. Although you may have the best starting hand, they might out-flop you. It's one of those damned-if-you-do and damned-if-you-don't situations.

When You Have a Medium Stack

With a medium stack, why would you ever be in a hurry? At a six-handed final table you should be able to get to the top three unless you take a horrible beat along the way. So you can wait until you're in the top three before you really open up and play. Until then you want to play conservatively. You would be more prone to gamble with a short stack than you would with a medium stack.

Look at it as though you're just starting out in a tournament playing at a full table. The antes and blinds won't be hurting you too much, so you're going to be pretty selective about the hands you play. You're just going to play the premium hands you're supposed to play.

Suppose you have a medium stack and the aggressive chip leader is sitting to your left. Since he gets to act after you, he's probably calling raises and making raises with cards that aren't necessarily big hands. If the man with the chips is on your left—and if he's an aggressive player—when you raise a pot, you must have a hand that can stand a reraise. Otherwise don't waste any money on the hand, throw it away.

At some time or another, a player is going to go on a rush in a tournament. Suppose you have an average stack (or even a big stack) and see that somebody's holding the deck. Maybe he hasn't held any cards for a long time and has just survived on guile and guts. Suddenly, he starts holding hands. Why would you, or any of his other opponents, want to go up against him? I saw it happen at the Four Queens Classic in 2004. In seven hands, David Ulliott had aces twice, queens once, and A-K once.

When you see people holding these kinds of hands, why play a pot with them? Wait for things to cool down a little and then you can play with them. The bottom line is, never play anybody's rush for him. Sometimes you'll see a player tangle with somebody on a rush, thinking that he can't have a good hand every time. Wrong. While the rush is on, whether he starts with the best hand doesn't matter—he catches the cards he needs. That's why I give players on a rush a wide path. But boy, when I see that the rush is over, I'm coming.

When You Have a Commanding Lead

When you have the biggest stack at the final table in six-handed action, everybody wants to get a piece of your chips. While they may be afraid of tangling with you, at the same time they are targeting you because you have what they need—chips. They can win only so much from their primary target, the short stack, but they can win a lot more chips from you if they beat you in a big pot. Be leery of them. While you want to build your lead even bigger, you still need to protect it by playing good poker.

I've seen players start with big stacks and blow their lead by playing recklessly, calling with trash hands like 8-5, or raising with weak hands like J-7 suited. "I've got some chips now," inexperienced players with big stacks sometimes think, "so I'll break this player and then I'll break that guy." That's not a good way to go about playing a big stack. You might get broke yourself in the process, so don't ever shoot for any one man. Let the flow of the game take its course.

It isn't like you're just starting the tournament when you have a huge lead to start with. You can take chances that your opponents can't afford to take. Say that they aren't usually bringing it in for a big raise; they're taking cheap flops. In that case you can see a lot of flops when you have a ton of chips. If it isn't a raised pot to start with, it won't cost you much to see the flop and it won't dent your stack much if you lose the hand.

You can open up your game when you have a big lead, just don't open it up too much. You can play the trap hands you were folding earlier on—hands like

K-J, Q-J, J-10—so long as it doesn't cost you too much to play a pot. You can call a standard raise with somewhat mediocre hands when you are in position, but avoid calling too often with them.

Remember that you don't want to double up the short stacks, and you certainly don't want to double up the medium stacks, so you need to have some kind of a hand when you play with them. If a short stack doubles up two or three times, he will have enough ammunition to do some harm. And if a medium stack doubles through you once or twice, you may find yourself trading places with him. Believe me, you don't want to end up on the short end of the stick by playing too loose.

If you have a huge lead, I can understand your being very aggressive. But I also believe that you should not be taking unnecessary chances and losing a lot of chips when you know the other guys with short and medium stacks are going to be trying their best to build their stacks to catch up with you. Make sure that you don't fall into the trap of playing policeman when you're in the blind. In other words, don't think that you have to call with any two cards just because you're the big stack and have a chance to knock out an opponent who has a small stack.

With the big stack at the final table, you have to play sort of "in and out" poker—play aggressively some of the time and conservatively some of the time. Be willing to play the bully in the right situations, but draw back your horns and retreat to the trenches when you have to.

When the Starting Stacks are Fairly Even

I've seen final tables where there isn't $20,000 difference in the chip counts from the number one spot to the sixth spot. If the stacks are pretty even at the start of the final table, it's a different ballgame. It's anybody's game. So, you have to play a lot differently from the way you would play if one player has a lot of chips and another player has very few chips, and the rest of the stacks are in the middle.

When everybody has almost even stacks, you don't play "final-table" poker, you play "real" poker just like you would play in a cash game. You don't play according to your stack size because nobody has a chip advantage. Any advantage you have in even-chip situations comes from your table position, not the number of chips you have. Play good hands in position and seize every situation you can to take advantage of your opponents. Bluff here and there when you believe it's the right move.

In summary, your final-table strategy partly depends on the distribution of the chips among you and your opponents. If the chips are pretty evenly distributed, play cash-game hold'em. If they're way out of kilter and you have the shortest stack, don't let yourself get anted out. Look for the first opportunity to get your money in with the best hand. With a medium stack, play a patient and controlled game. With a large stack, try to control the table without playing recklessly.

PART 8

Three-Handed and Heads Up at the Final Table

The money, the title and the glory are on the line. With your skill and strategy, plus a little luck, you can grab the brass ring.

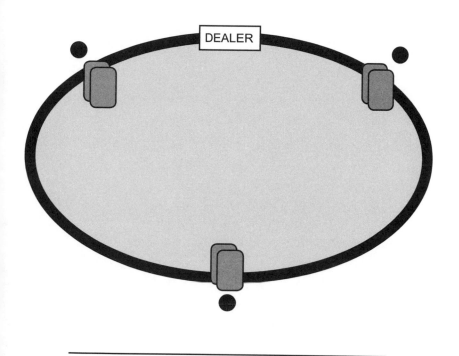

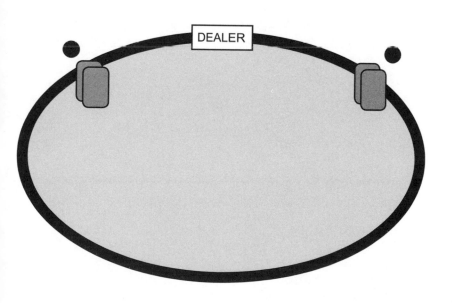

The stronger the competition, the more I enjoy playing three-handed. In the 2001 World Series of Poker $2,500 no-limit hold'em tournament, I had the rare opportunity of playing against two world-class players whose abilities I highly respect, Phil Hellmuth and Layne Flack. The three of us are all pretty good players, so this tournament is a good example of how top players play each other three-handed.

In one particular pot (one that Phil likes to talk about), Layne raised the pot in the little blind with K-K and Phil called him with an A-6 offsuit. The flop came with Q-2-6. In an attempt to trap Phil, Layne checked his overpair. Phil checked behind him. When a 9 hit the board on the turn, Layne checked again to lure Phil into his trap. Phil took the bait and bet $25,000. Layne then raised him $50,000 more and Phil called the raise, although I don't know how he could've thought that he had the best hand. Phil got extremely lucky when another 6 came on the river. Layne bet $140,000 all-in, and naturally, Phil called with trip sixes and sent Layne out the door in third place.

Even though great players will call raises before the flop with an ace-small when the action is three-handed, Phil thought that he also made a great play by calling Layne's reraise on the turn. I disagree. What did he think he could beat against Layne's check-raise? Of course, he caught the right card on the river to win the pot—and there's nothing wrong with getting lucky. This was the key pot when we were three-handed, and it gave Phil a huge lead over me in our heads-up play. Phil finished first and I took second.

The next year in the $2,500 no-limit hold'em WSOP tournament, I got an incredible second chance to compete against two top players. This time it was Johnny Chan, Layne and I. This was the strangest final table I've ever seen, simply because of the number of big hands that were dealt. Usually when you see the hands turned up on the end, one player has a real hand and the other has a lesser holding. But earlier in the action at this final table, Layne flopped quad nines and beat Phil Marmorstein's quad fours to send him out in fourth place. Carlos Mortensen had already gone out in fifth place with pocket eights when I had A-Q and flopped a higher pair.

I had just taken the lead three-handed and looked down at the A♠ K♠. Layne brought it in for a raise and I moved him in. Layne didn't hesitate to call with pocket nines. Since I was sitting to his left, I had gone over the top of him many times in this tournament—you have to play pretty aggressively against Layne because he's very aggressive himself. This time he decided to take a stand. "What was I gonna do?" he told me later on. "Try to grind it out with you and Johnny?" He knew that his nines were either an 11 to 10 favorite or a 4.5 to 1 underdog before he called. Layne flopped a nine to win a huge pot in what turned out to be the key hand for me.

About two hands later, I was dealt another big hand, two aces. I moved in. Johnny Chan called me with an A-K, and I doubled up, but not to the point where I had a lot of chips. I had over $100,000, but they both had a lot more than that. A few hands later, Layne raised before the flop and I moved all in with an A-Q. Three-handed, A-Q is a big-big hand. Johnny called and so did Layne. Guess what they had? They both had an A-K! You just don't see hands like this come up very often playing short-handed. It was overkill when they caught a king on the board to race me out of the tournament in third place. Layne went on to win it with Johnny coming second.

Both these tournaments are good examples of top players battling it out with each other in three-way action. They are my way of introducing you to the exciting and treacherous world of three-handed play in big tournaments. Now, here are some tips on how to play four-handed, three-handed and heads-up no-limit hold'em.

WHEN YOU'RE PLAYING FOUR-HANDED OR THREE-HANDED

The most important considerations in three-handed play are who you're playing against and your chip position. You pretty much know the caliber of your opponents by the time you get short-handed because you've been playing with them ever since you started at the final table. But playing against two or three top players like I did in the examples above doesn't happen all the time. Usually the player mix is different.

For example, in the 2005 World Series of Poker $5,000 buy-in no-limit hold'em tournament, I played three-handed against John Bonetti, a top pro, and Steve Zoine, a brand new tournament player. And that mix made it a different ball game. Bonetti and I had been playing together since we were pups, but I had never played against Zoine before the final table began. He had held the hands and won the pots, and had the chip lead most of the way—and he didn't have any fear whatsoever.

So I had to play against him in a different way than I would a seasoned veteran of final-table action. I didn't try to get real fancy against Zoine; instead I usually played him pretty straightforwardly. (You'll find several of the hands we played together illustrated in the next chapter.)

Adjust to Your Opponents' Style of Play

You must play your opponents differently according to their style of play and their level of experience. Against new players you must figure out if they're passive, aggressive, or some place in the middle of the road. If you notice that a man is very passive, you can play aggressively against him in shorthanded action. If you know that he won't call reraises unless he has a huge hand, even though you're playing shorthanded, you have to take advantage of that. Let him know that every time he sticks a chip in the pot, you are liable to go over the top of him.

Or suppose you have a really good player at the table, as I did when I played Stu Ungar heads-up in three major tournaments in the old days. He couldn't stand two checks, but he was still a very good player, maybe the best. I might check twice and then he would bet, I would go over the top of him, and he would throw his hand away because he didn't want to lose any more money to the hand. And the few times that he called me when I went over the top, I really had a hand, so it worked out perfectly for me. I knew the caliber of player he was, and he understood the quality of my play, so we showed a lot of respect for each other.

Some players seem to think that I bluff quite a bit, but actually I don't bluff very often, and Ungar knew that. Actually I play pretty solid poker most of the time, adjusting my game when I need to. I can be very

171

aggressive or I might be passive depending on the situation. I'm not afraid to put my money in the pot and then throw my hand away if I think I'm beaten.

Adjusting to your opponent's style is so important because it gives you the upper hand against him. For example, Antonio Esfandiari was sitting on my right at the big tournament at the Sands in Atlantic City. He is a very aggressive player, but I had position over him.

Every time Antonio made a move I came over the top of him. I showed him that he wasn't going to be able to run over me, and it worked; I had him looking up at the sky for help. Afterwards, Antonio told me that he learned something from this experience. He hasn't lost any of his aggression, but he said that he's only going to use it against certain people. In other words, he's going to play his opponent more often.

And that's the point of this story: You must learn how to adapt your style to the style that works best against your opponents. If they're passive, you become aggressive. If they're very aggressive, sometimes you have to play overly aggressive and come over the top of them. But only up to a point—you don't want to be a fool, either. You simply want to take their edge away from them and put it in your court.

Your Chip Count

When you get to three-handed, everyone usually has plenty of chips to play with. Therefore unless you're by far the short stack, the same rules apply as when you were playing six-handed. You want to be aggressive, you want to dictate the action, but you don't want to make foolish plays trying to take control of the table. And sometimes you get into a situation like I did in 2001 and 2002 where it's very hard to dictate the action because you're up against two top players who are trying to dictate it at the same time.

By then the blinds and antes are pretty heavy, so if you're the short stack you just have to find a hand you like and get your chips in. But suppose the stacks are fairly evenly matched. Are you going to try to outplay your opponents? I don't figure I'm going to outplay players the caliber of Chan or Flack. The pros are going to play top-notch poker, which makes it very hard to make moves on them. You might want to sit back and wait for good situations against them, and seize every opportunity as it comes up. And if you can't outplay them, you'd better hope that you out-hold them.

Your Table Position

When you're playing three-handed, you're always in the small blind, the big blind or on the button. Every time you're on the button, obviously you have the upper hand because you get to act last after the flop. But realize that your opponents are going to play with you, so you can't make your standard raise before the flop to either force your opponents out, or to build a big pot. When I say "standard raise," I mean that the first raise made at each level becomes the standard raise for that round of play, usually three to five times the big blind in a full ring. But the blinds and antes are way up there in three-handed play, so instead of raising five times the big blind, you might raise ten times the big blind. Make them pay to play with you, or force them out if they have a marginal hand.

At the beginning of each level, I set my own standard raise. I let them do what they want to do, but I raise the amount that I need to raise in order to get called, or to get my opponent to fold his hand. Over 90 percent of the time I raise, I want to get called because I think I have the best hand. The other times, I'm bluffing.

Because players have a lot of chips at this stage, they're going to call a lot of small raises. If you're going to raise, make it enough that they have to think about calling you with just an average hand. You don't want them calling with hands like J-10 when you have a medium pair. But they will call if you just make a standard raise because, with plenty of chips, they want to play pots with you. Keep the pressure on them all the time. When you raise, raise big. Let them have to call you for some real money. It works.

Making a big raise doesn't mean that you should move all in. Say that you move in with 10-10. What's to say that someone doesn't have J-J or better? But you've moved all in, so now you have to play the hand through. So just make a decent raise, don't commit your entire stack to the hand. That way, if they come back over the top of you, you've given yourself an opportunity to decide whether you want to continue with the hand. That's what poker is all about, making the right decisions. By not going all in, you give yourself a second chance. But when you're all in against a bigger stack, you'd better win the pot or you're all out.

Remember that when you're the button, you're out of position before the flop because you have to act first. You have to think about that and play accordingly. Suppose you're the button with something like 7-5 and decide, "Well, it's about time I picked up a pot. I'm raising." But picking up the pot might not be quite as easy as you think. You don't have any inkling of what your opponents have because they haven't acted yet. You're the first to act, so it takes that "button" move out of play. Before the flop the big blind has the position of power because he gets to act last. After the flop the button has the point of power. This shift in power changes things quite a bit.

A lot of stealing goes on when you're playing heads-up. Two-handed the small blind is on the button and has to act first before the flop. So when you're the small blind heads-up, you can do a lot of moving in and putting your opponent to the test—even though you're the first to act. But in three-handed play with two people sitting behind you, things are a little different. Sure, you can still do some stealing, but you can't do as much of it because you have to get two guys out of the pot rather than only one.

The Quality of Your Hands

When you're three-handed, the quality of hands you play somewhat depends on the nature of your opponents. Playing three-handed, I know a pro that brings in a king-anything for a raise if the pot hasn't been raised. If he's on the button (first to act) with a K-x, he raises. He knows that a king-high hand is better than a random hand in three-handed action, and he plays it stronger than I do. Knowing that, I can use it against him when we play together. If I believe that he's been raising a lot of pots with random kings, I might go over the top of him to represent an ace or a pair.

Against Johnny Chan I play differently. Johnny doesn't pick up as many pots as a lot of people do, but don't think that he won't try to steal one every now and then. He doesn't attempt to steal as often; he tries to play a hand. He understands that the value of hands changes in three-handed play. And he's very good at trapping his opponents.

When you're playing three-handed, your starting hand standards aren't nearly as high as when you're playing six-handed. The blinds and antes can eat you up playing three-handed because you're constantly putting them in, so you cannot afford to wait for premium hands like big pairs or A-K. You aren't going to be dealt aces, kings, queens and pairs very often, because only six cards are being taken off the deck. (Obviously the more cards dealt, the better your chances of getting a big hand.) Therefore any paint with a connecting card becomes a playable hand in shorthanded play—K-Q, K-J, K-10, Q-10, for example.

Hands like J-10 aren't bad cards three-handed. Of course if you get a lot of action on it, it's probably an underdog, but there are a lot worse hands than J-10, and there are a lot of hands you can make with it. When I get J-10 and I'm first to act, I'm playing. I'm not saying that I'm raising with it, but I'm playing. And there are some situations where I will raise with it. There are two ways I can win: If they don't call, I win what's in the pot at the time; and if they do call, I probably have a live hand although I might be a dog to start with.

You don't want to play "three-holers" like K-9 or Q-8. The only three-hole connecting hand you can play is A-10, which is the only one you can make the nuts with if you flop a straight. If you flop a straight to any other connecting cards with three gaps, a higher straight will be possible. For example, if you have Q-8 and it comes J-10-9, you don't have the nuts. That's the problem with playing three-gap connecting cards, even in three-handed play.

In three-handed play, a pocket pair becomes a very

important hand—but it is not a move-in hand. People make their biggest mistake three-handed when they move all in with little pairs. If you keep moving in with small pairs, somebody is eventually going to pick up a hand that will beat you and you'll be gone. Make a standard raise with medium to baby pairs. Why would you risk all your chips by moving in with them?

I guess I'll always wonder why so many players always want to move in with their good hands. It just doesn't make sense to me. Suppose you have pocket threes and you move all in. Out of the blue one of your opponents decides, "I like this 9-8 suited. I'm gonna play!" He's only an 11 to 10 dog to your small pair. And if he hits one of his cards, you're a huge dog. There's a better way to do things. If you're going to move in, you want to have a nice hand, make a decent raise with it, and let them come back at you. Then get them. Get their money in there first so you can win something with your big pairs and high hands.

No-limit hold'em is not a move-in game—it's a play-five-cards game. As the board changes, you can do different things. You can actually outplay a man. I don't care if you're playing the two best players in the world, you can still outplay them on any individual hand. And they can outplay you on any particular hand. You just want to pick your spots carefully and avoid taking unnecessary risks.

Give yourself a chance to win the tournament; don't blow it by making a big-big mistake. And don't be afraid to play a hand through. I start wanting to play hands out from the very beginning of the tournament and all the way through it. If I move in, it's because I'm hoping to get called—or I'm hoping not to get called. It's one or the other. But it's up to my opponents to figure it out for themselves. Most of the time, though, I want to get called when I move in.

You have to figure out the starting hand standards of your opponents compared to your standards, and how they are playing their hands. You can find that out pretty quickly. Say you're playing three-handed and the other two are playing a hand. If those hands are shown down, you can learn something because you can see what they played and how they played it, and what price they paid to play it.

You will see people playing hands like K-3 or Q-8 suited. If they're playing K-3 suited and those kinds of hands, they don't want to get called. If they happen to get called, they're hoping they started with the best hand. Suited or not, big-little suited cards and three-gap hands spell trouble. I'm not saying that you have to throw them away every time, but realize that if you raise with that type of hand, it's because you're trying to win the pot right there. If you get called, you hope the flop comes queen or king high and your opponent doesn't have a king or queen.

If your opponent is raising with hands like 7-6 and 9-8 when you're playing three-handed or heads-up, obviously you have to adjust to that. You can't let him run over you, so you need to come over the top every now and then to slow him down and let him know that you're not going to put up with his trying to bully you. Just hope that's the kind of hand he has when you decide to play with him rather than a big pair.

Raising and Limping

Do you always bring in the pot for a raise at the final table when you're the first one in the pot? I've been asked that question a lot. The answer is no. One thing to consider before you raise is the number of opponents you have. Whereas K-Q is a trouble hand when you're playing nine-handed, it gains a lot of value when you're playing four-handed or three-handed. I might just limp in with it four-handed. Then if somebody raises, I'll have to decide whether he has a better hand than I have. Does he have an ace-something? A pair? If he has a pair, do I have two overcards? Or is it likely that I have the best hand? Mind games like these are a good reason for limping in with these types of hands, remembering that you don't really want to play a raised pot with them.

Be careful with your bluff raises. Hopefully your opponent will fold when you bluff. And a lot of times they do. But if you bluff raise or make a bluff bet to try to steal a pot, be leery if you get called. You have to be very careful when you're bluffing, because your opponents usually are going to call you a second time playing shorthanded. They wouldn't have made the first call if they weren't ready to play the hand.

Say that you raised with J-10 and the flop comes A-5-4. Now how do you play your jack? Do you take a shot at it and represent an ace? Or do you shut down, figuring they have an ace? You don't want to give up the money you've already put in the pot, but you also don't want to lose any more to it than you have to. You're damned if you do and damned if you don't.

Limping into pots is okay so long as you don't make a big habit of doing it. If your opponents get accustomed to seeing you throw hands away against a raise, they will take advantage of you every time you limp. Once in a while, limp in with a huge hand. Then if they want to play back at you, you like it.

Now let's take a look at how you might play in three-way action when you're the short stack and when you're the big stack.

When You're the Short Stack

Suppose you're the shortest stack three-handed. If your opponents have $500,000 each and you have $400,000, it's still a game. For example, at the 2000 WSOP final table when I started with the shortest stack, the blinds weren't so high that I couldn't play. And because of that, I formulated a game plan. (God, I wish I'd won that thing!)

But say that your opponents have $500,000 each and you have less than $100,000, making you by far the shortest stack. Now you're playing a move-in game. Any pot you play, you have to play for all your chips. That is, unless you have a huge hand and you want to suck them into the pot. But generally speaking, any hand that you play, you play for your whole stack. Let's say that you have a K-J. What are you going to do? If you only have $100,000, the blinds are probably $5,000-$10,000 plus the ante. You can't just flat-call with it. So are you going to raise $20,000 or $30,000? That's not a big enough raise to force anybody out, so you have to move in with the hand if you're going to play it.

If somebody has limped in front of you, you can just call with your K-J. But if you're the first player to act, you have to raise with it. When you move all in, the other stacks know that you've found something you want to play. That is, unless you have only $50,000 with $10,000-$20,000 blinds. In that case, they know that you're going to move in with any two cards, no matter what they are. Winning the pot is your only chance to stay in the action. You do not want to get anted out. That's a no-no.

When You're the Big Stack

If you have the big stack, now's the time when you can start becoming the bully. You're into the big money, which is what you've been shooting for, and you have the lead in chips. You can put them to the test at any time. You want to dictate the action, especially the action that you're involved in. You want to be the dictator, not the caller. If you're first to act, bring it in for a raise. That way your opponents never know where you're coming from; they don't know whether you have a hand or are on a steal.

I used to watch the great Bobby Hoff play heads-up in Vegas in the old days. He kept the pressure on his opponents a hundred percent of the time. They never knew where Bobby was coming from, but they knew that if they put a dime in the pot, they were going to get raised. If you can keep them befuddled, you can beat them. Hoff is a master of the art.

Practice

Sit-and-go tournaments and heads-up matches are very good places to practice. I frequently play in sit-and-go tournaments online. That's where I like to practice my head-up game. I find that the aggressor wins maybe 75 percent of the time. The guy who just waits for a hand might win about 25 percent of the time. The thing that can hurt you when you're the aggressor is this—you might win 75 percent of the pots, but your opponent might win all the big pots. So, it doesn't matter that you won all those little hands because when the big pot comes along, you're a goner if he wins it. This is what has happened in a lot of heads-up matches over the years. Play a few online sit-and-go tournaments and you'll see what I mean.

PLAYING HEADS-UP

Heads-up play is a match of wits. You're playing more of a mind game than a card game when you get heads-up. The cards are in front of you, but the play is more in your mind than it is in the cards you hold. It's which cards you play, when you play them, and how you play them that count. You know how your opponent plays. Now it's up to you to meet the challenge and outplay him when the chips are down and your tournament life is on the line.

If you get 50 percent of the cards, can you win with them? When I say 50 percent, I mean that if you get half the deck and he gets the other half, the cards break even. When the cards break even, are you good enough to win? That's the competitive part. If two great players are heads-up, that's really a terrific match. But say that somebody new to the game is playing against a very experienced player. If the cards break even, the experienced player should win every single time.

Old-timers like Goody Roy, Jack Straus, and Everett Goulsby were great heads-up players. Jack couldn't play a ring game worth a damn, but he had all the right moves heads-up. If he had a middle-buster straight draw, he was liable to put you all in with it. You just never knew where he was coming from. But in a ring, he was a stone fish. If he put his name up on the board to start a game, everybody wanted to play with him. Everett used to go around boasting that he was the best heads-up player, and there's no doubt that he was great at it. "I played Straus three times heads-up," he told us, "and I beat him all three times." So I went to Jack a couple of weeks later and asked him about Everett's brag. "Bullshit!" Straus said. "I won all three times and it's chronicled."

Whether Jack or Everett was right, here are some tips that will help you feel the thrill of victory rather than the agony of defeat. I've felt both emotions in heads-up battle. And win or lose, I have been greatly rewarded financially. But believe me when I tell you that nothing compares to the overwhelming high of winning a big tournament.

The Cards You Play

Remember that only four cards are coming off the deck when you're heads-up, leaving a whole lot of cards still in the deck. As you go down the line from 10-handed to six-handed to three-handed to heads up, it takes a progressively weaker hand to win. The smaller the number of players, the smaller the hand it takes to win. The more players, the bigger the hand it takes to win since more cards are out of the deck. Just don't get carried away with this concept and figure that you can get away with playing any two cards. You still must maintain a feel for hand values and set starting-hand standards for yourself.

An ace is a very powerful card in heads-up play, but I'm leery of most "medium" aces. Although an

A-8, A-7, or A-6 will win most of the time against an A-2, A-3, A-4, or A-5, I would rather play an ace with a low connector against a random hand without an ace because it has the possibility of making a straight, whereas you can't do that with an ace and a middle card.

Just remember that if you make a raise with a medium ace and get called, there's a good chance that your opponent has a bigger kicker. He probably won't have an A-K or A-Q unless he's trying to trap you. But he might have A-J, in which case he'll probably come over the top of you. Or he could have any of the other aces that are better than yours, so you have to be very leery. And there will be a lot of times when your opponent tries to trap you. If you're very aggressive and raise all the time, your opponent is likely to just flat-call you if he has an A-K because he wants to get all your chips. However, if I have A-K I will come back over the top 95 percent of the time, hoping that I have the best hand.

Pairs are also important. You're going to play almost any pair, plus the other combinations I mentioned. You don't want to play hands like 9-8, 9-7, or 8-7 (the middle connectors). If your opponent has a big chip lead, he will put the pressure on you if he sees that you're playing these types of hands. So, keep the hands you play to pairs and paints. And play them strong. You always want to be in control of any situation.

Of course there are scenarios where you might be tempted to play a middle pair stronger than you should. A disastrous hand that my writing partner, Tom McEvoy, played against Mimi Tran in the National Heads-Up televised tournament is an excellent example of what I'm talking about. Tom had $25,000 in chips and Mimi had $15,000 when she moved all in. Holding 7-7, Tom called in a heartbeat.

At first glance this looks like the right play, but after further analysis, you will see that even if Mimi had 9-8 offsuit, she still would be only an 11 to 10 underdog. She actually held the Q♥ 10♥ and spiked a queen to win the pot and severely cripple Tom's stack. So, in keeping with the concept of being in control, this play does not look as good as it did at first glance. You want to be a big favorite when you put a lot of chips in the pot in this kind of situation.

Should you play every hand? No. You do pass quite often in heads-up play. You don't see all the passes on televised tournaments, because they only choose the big-action hands to broadcast. In that sense, televised tournaments do not give you a true picture of the actual play when it gets to heads-up. In live games, you'll see guys playing any two cards heads up. If they get a middle buster straight draw, they're liable to move in to keep the pressure on you. But in a tournament where you're playing for a lot more prize money, it's different. Of course you still have to be willing to play. And you have to seize every single situation.

You cannot let the other man get the upper hand on you. You both have so many chips, if you let him get the upper hand he's going to beat you in every pot, just chipping away at you. Sooner or later, you're going to pick up a hand, but if he's already taken a lot of chips away from you, it can be pretty hard to catch up. And if he can get away from a hand when you finally play, you don't win much. You have to at least match his level of aggression in the play of your hands. And then use your brains.

Your Position at the Table

Like it is all the way through poker, the button is the position of power. When you're on the button (the small blind in heads-up play), you're first to act before the flop but you're last to act after the flop. When you have the button and raise before the flop, you're out of position since you're the first to act. But if your opponent calls the raise, you will be in position after the flop. Use that in your favor. Any time you're in the big blind, you have the worst of it because the other guy has position on you. So your hand standards are lower when you have the button than they are when you're in the big blind. That is, the hands you choose to play or raise with on the button can be more varied. For example, I might raise with Q-J or Q-10 when I have the button heads-up.

Going All In

Do you go all-in a lot? If you have a big hand, you do. Say that you have an A-Q—that's a big hand in heads-up play. Boom! You're moving in. And you're hoping to get called. If you don't get called, you win the antes and blinds. And those antes and blinds are so large at this stage that they mean something. If you can win 10 blinds, you've won a lot of chips. I've raised 10 times in a row playing heads-up and seen my opponent throw his hand away every time. That can give you a big edge. Of course if you're playing against a super-aggressive player, there's no way you're going to get away with raising 10 times in a row. He's going to come over the top of you, and you have to be ready for that.

You know how your opponents have been playing at the final table, and you formulate your heads-up plan for playing against them as the table gets shorter. That's what I do. "If I get heads-up with this guy, how am I going to play him?" I figure. Like a bridge or chess player, I want to be five steps ahead of him. I'm like a pilot thinking ahead of the plane so that I don't fly into a mountain. I want to be ready for him when heads-up play begins, so I'm formulating my plan as we go along at the final table.

But some players are pretty tricky—they change their style of play as the table gets shorter. You've seen your opponent play from the start of the final table, so you know his usual modus operandi. This knowledge should make it easier for you to recognize when he makes the shift. He may have played one way at the start of the final table, but started playing completely different in short-handed play, like Dr. Jekyl and Mr. Hyde. Maybe your opponent has played squeaky tight all the way through but started opening up his game, playing almost every hand, when three-way or heads-up action began. With a chameleon-like player, it's tougher to execute the plan you've formulated for playing against him heads-up. But if you want to win, you have to be able to adjust to his new colors. This is what I mean about heads-up play being a mind game.

When You're the Short Stack

Truthfully, I don't mind having the lesser amount of chips when I first start playing heads-up. I don't want my opponent to have a 10 to 1 chip lead on me, like Ferguson had over me in 2000. But still, you can chip away at your opponent pretty well with a short stack because you have a lot of chips when it gets to heads-up play. The other guy may have a lot more, but you still have plenty of chips to play with, depending on the size of the blinds. If I have $200,000 with $5,000-$10,000 blinds, I'm comfortable. I don't care if my opponent has $2 million, I'm going to come after him. That's no time to give up.

If you're really short-stacked—maybe you took a bad beat just before heads-up play started—you want to go all in as soon as you can. When you decide to play a hand, you want to play it for all your chips. You would love to get back to even par with your opponent because then you can really start playing cards. That's why you have to open up when you're really short-stacked and then hope for the best. Even if you have the worst of it, you hope to win pots. You have to get lucky sometime in the tournament, whether you're a pro or an amateur, or you're not going to get there. That's all there is to it.

In a Bellagio tournament, I took a stand with the Q♠ 10♠ against my opponent's offsuit K-Q. I brought it in for $400 and he made it $1,400 to go. I called the raise. If I hadn't taken that stand, I wouldn't have gone as deep as I did. The flop came Q-10-4 and he went bust with top pair and top kicker against my two pair.

Usually I wouldn't have played the hand to start with, and I definitely wouldn't have stood a raise with it. But I thought that the time had come for me to open up and play while I still had some chips to play with. Four times during the first hour of play, I had been dealt K-Q suited and didn't play the hand because I was out of position. I'm always afraid I'm going to flop one pair to the hand, get in the action, and my opponent will have the ace kicker to beat me. Yet Mimi Tran played it one time, the flop came J-10-9, and she doubled up with it. It's almost unbelievable how important your timing is in playing no-limit hold'em.

In Summary

Playing heads-up for the championship is the time when all your observation and other powers come into play. You finally get to test everything that you've learned about your single opponent. Do you have it right or do you have it wrong? Will the cards help you defeat him? After all is said and done, the cards have to cooperate.

It all comes together when you get heads up. You finally get your true test in finding out whether you're correct in your evaluations. Now is when your mind game is at it its peak performance. And that's the fun part. We all play for the money, but we also like the thrill of beating somebody. I've been competitive all my life and that's what it all boils down to—I want to beat him!

I don't get excited playing in the side games any more, or in the little tournaments—but when I'm in a big tournament and I get heads-up, I'm like a little kid who just got his first red lollipop. I'm ready to play!

PART 9

The Anatomy of a Championship Table

A Play-by-Play Analysis of the Final Table
At the 2005 World Series of Poker
$5,000 No-limit Hold'em Tournament

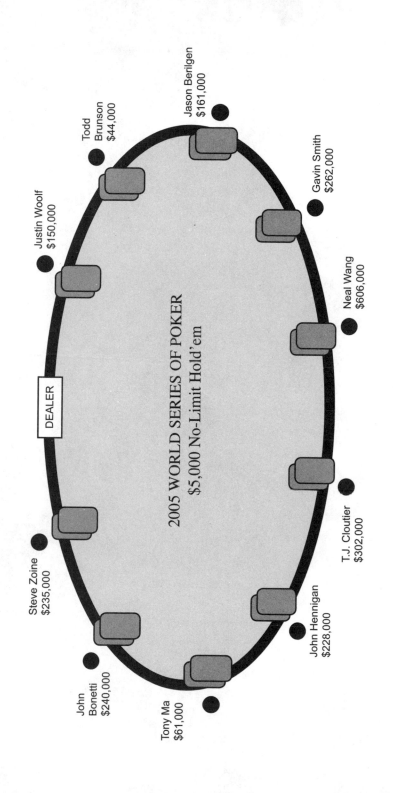

2005 WORLD SERIES OF POKER
$5,000 No-Limit Hold'em

DEALER

Justin Woolf
$150,000

Todd
Brunson
$44,000

Jason Berilgen
$161,000

Gavin Smith
$262,000

Neal Wang
$606,000

T.J. Cloutier
$302,000

John Hennigan
$228,000

Tony Ma
$61,000

John
Bonetti
$240,000

Steve Zoine
$235,000

I have dedicated the preceding chapters of this book to defining my thoughts and suggestions on playing a tournament from four tables through the final table. In this chapter I will share my thoughts and observations of an actual World Series of Poker tournament I played, how the players were eliminated, and what we perhaps could have done differently. First, I'll give you the tournament facts. Then I'll introduce the final table players, their chip counts, seat position, and a few comments on each of them.

The $5,000 no-limit hold'em tournament at the 2005 WSOP, which is second in prestige only to the championship event, began with 466 players and paid 45 places. The total prize pool was $2,190,200 with a top prize of $667,100. ESPN filmed our play at the championship table, with Lon McEachern and Norman Chad doing the commentary for the nationally broadcast coverage. If you videotaped the tournament when it was shown on ESPN, you can follow along with most of the hands I discuss in this section.

At the start of the broadcast, the commentators

described John Bonetti and me as "venerable veterans" at the final table, contrasting us with the younger players who appeared at many of the other final tables at the 2005 WSOP. Referring to 77-year-old Bonetti, Chad joked, "For once, T.J. is not the oldest player at the table." Bonetti said it was a match-up between "the old elephants and the young lions."

Here is my description of the lineup. What I have written about the players is a practice that I repeat mentally every time I reach a final table. This time I was facing five players that I had played with many times, and four players I didn't know very well.

SEAT 1:
JUSTIN "NEVER WIN" WOOLF
$150,000 in eighth chip position—

I had heard that Justin was a very successful online player, someone I would have to watch to see how his game developed. After placing fifty-ninth out of 826 in a $1,000 WSOP no-limit hold'em event earlier, Justin went on to win fourth place in the $2,000 no-limit hold'em tournament a few days after he played this $5,000 tournament.

SEAT 2:
TODD BRUNSON
$44,000 in tenth chip position—

As far as I am concerned, Todd is one of the world's best all-around poker players. He defeated me at the Mirage heads-up no-limit hold'em tournament in 2005. A week after this $5,000 no-limit tournament, Todd went on to win his first WSOP bracelet in the $2500 Omaha high-low event.

SEAT 3:
JASON "DOC" BERILGEN
$161,000 in seventh chip position—

A physician from Houston, the young doctor had finished in the money for $40,000 in his only other big buy-in tournament, a World Poker Tour event.

SEAT 4:
GAVIN SMITH
$262,000 in third chip position—

A very talented young player from Canada, Gavin has an excellent track record in no-limit hold'em tournaments. He has placed in several WPT events, and had just won a major tournament in Las Vegas the month before the Series began. I have played with him many times.

SEAT 5:
NEAL WANG
$606,000 in first chip position—

The chip leader at the start of the championship table, Neal is a very good poker player. After we got down to two tables, he chose to sit on his chips and not play very many hands.

SEAT 6:
T. J. CLOUTIER
$302,000 in second chip position—

In his excellent write-up on the tournament, WSOP Media Director Nolan Dalla wrote a line that I sincerely appreciate: "Just like fine wine, T.J. Cloutier gets better with age." As I told Nolan in our post-tournament interview, "I'm not ready for the pasture just yet. I still have a few more wins left in me. John Bonetti was here tonight and he's 12 years older than me, so maybe I can still be doing it when I'm his age. Compared to him, I'm still a kid."

SEAT 7:
JOHN "WORLD" HENNIGAN
$228,000 in sixth chip position—

A great high-limit poker player, John is known for being super-aggressive. He won the H.O.R.S.E. event at the WSOP in 2002 and won a second bracelet in the limit hold'em event in 2004. John and I played together heads-up at the World Heads-up Championship broadcast on NBC television.

SEAT 8:
TONY MA
$61,000 in ninth chip position—

A two-time bracelet winner at the WSOP, "Tony the Tiger" is always in the thick of things in no-limit hold'em tournaments. He really knows how to play well in the later stages of a tournament.

SEAT 9:
JOHN BONETTI
$240,000 in fourth chip position—

Bonetti has three WSOP bracelets and is well known for his brash and aggressive nature anytime he plays. Dalla described him as a "cantankerous curmudgeon." He and I have been playing together for ages, and John has only gotten better as the years go by.

SEAT 10:
STEVE ZOINE
$235,000 in fifth chip position—

Although a newcomer to the WSOP tournament scene, Steve has a lot of natural talent. He usually seemed to make the right move at the right time, except for one hand that is detailed later in this chapter.

Having a book on every opponent is a must in tournament poker. Your book will at least give you a basic understanding of their play. And take it from me, a leopard can't change its spots. Your opponents may vary their style for a while, but inevitably they will revert to what brought them this far, their own basic style. Against players you have not played with before, pay attention and you will soon be able to see what category they fit into, and then play them accordingly. Add their names to your book so that the next time you meet up with them, you'll know their style of play.

Now let's take a look at several of the key hands we played at the final table. Hopefully you will gain some insights into what it takes to win the championship.

2005 WSOP $5,000 No-Limit Hold'em
10-Handed at the Final Table
"The Refrigerator Hand"
T.J. Cloutier versus Gavin Smith

All of the WSOP telecasts feature a "Hold'em or Fold'em" hand. They show the hole cards of two players, plus the board cards. Then they pause the telecast and zoom in on a group of college-age kids who are watching the tournament on TV. When the TV announcer gives him his cue—"What would you do? Would you hold'em or fold'em?"—one of the actors dashes over to a refrigerator for another beer. Inside the fridge, Chris Ferguson is crouching. "What do you think, Chris? Hold'em or fold'em?" the actor asks. Chris' answer is either one or the other.

With 10 players still in action at the final table, the "refrigerator hand" of our tournament came up. Gavin Smith, who had started in third chip position, had lost most of his chips a few hands earlier to John

Hennigan when he lost a big pot with an A-Q against Hennigan's A-K. As the result, Hennigan catapulted to second chip position and Smith fell down the ladder from third position to around the sixth rung.

Gavin raised the pot before the flop with the 9♣ 9♠. I called him with the A♣ Q♣. The flop came 5♦ 6♦ 4♠ and Gavin checked it to me. I checked behind him. "I'll bet he has a middle pair," I said to myself. "If I hit an ace or a queen, I know I'll have the best hand. But if a king or a jack comes on the turn card, I'm going to lead at this hand." I knew that Gavin was playing very conservatively at the time and wouldn't call me because of the beat he had taken against Hennigan.

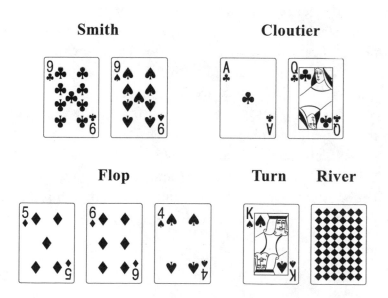

Smith   Cloutier

Flop   Turn   River

When the K♠ came off on fourth street, it was just perfect for me. He checked again and I fired in a $50,000 bet, since I had already planned to bet if anything came off the deck on fourth street that I could represent.

At this point in the TV coverage, the cameras focused in on the actors in the fictitious home game and the kid rushed to the refrigerator to ask Chris' opinion. "Hold'em!" Chris advised.

Too bad Gavin couldn't hear him. He folded. My plan had worked.

Gavin had around $100,000 left in his chip stack when I bet the $50,000, which was plenty of chips to play with since the blinds were only $3,000-$6,000. If he had been very low on chips, I probably would not have bet at all. Why? Because if he had been very short-stacked, he could have been in the mood to think, "I raised before the flop and T.J. just called, so I might as well go ahead with my hand since there's only one overcard on board."

I fired in a bet because I knew that Gavin realized that he still had plenty of chips left to play with, and most likely would think, "Why should I make a long call in this spot when I have enough chips to wait for a better situation?" All these things were going through my mind so I made the play that I thought the situation deserved.

When he checked on the flop, Gavin probably hoped that I would fire at the pot right there so that he could come over the top with his overpair. But once the king came out on the turn, it changed the whole situation. If our hands had been reversed—if he had the A-Q and I had the two nines—I would have led on the flop. That way, if my opponent had wanted to make a play at me, at least I would've had money in the pot and could decide whether I wanted to go on with the hand or fold it. And there would've been a pretty good chance that he would throw his hand away. I never want to give my opponent a chance to make a play that I made at him—and then turn it back on me. So, I would've played the hand a little differently than Gavin did.

The next hand that Gavin and I played together was his last. I raised $20,000 from early position before the flop with the 10♣ 8♣. It was an unusual play on my part, I know, but all I was hoping to do was pick up the antes. And if I got called, I figured I would have two live cards against any hand. Everybody folded to Gavin, who called all-in from the big blind with the 10♠ 7♥. "You've got me," I said, but when we turned over our hands, I saw that I had him out-kicked. The board came 8♦ K♠ A♦ J♠ 3♦. The flop had sealed his fate, and Gavin exited in tenth place $24,090 richer.

2005 WSOP $5,000 No-Limit Hold'em
9-Handed at the Final Table
T.J. Cloutier, Tony Ma and John Hennigan

In this key hand, Tony Ma, who had been short-chipped all the way, went all in with the A♦ K♦. I called with the 3♥ 3♣ and John Hennigan called behind me with the 4♠ 4♣. The flop came 7♠ 3♠ 10♦. I fired in a bet with my set of threes and Hennigan folded. The turn card was the 6♦ followed by the 2♣ on the river to eliminate Ma from the tournament. The two-time bracelet winner put close to $43,805 in his pocket before heading for home.

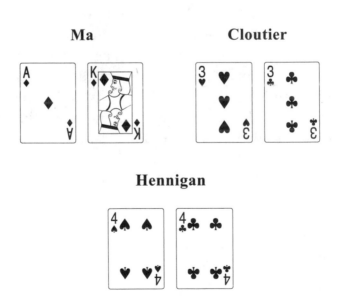

Ma   **Cloutier**

Hennigan

Flop   **Turn**   **River**

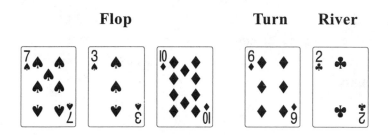

Why did I bet into a dry pot? Hennigan was on my left and had stood a raise behind me before the flop. I led at the pot on the flop because I wanted him to call me. A lot of times, leading at a pot when one man is all-in will force the other player to call you. It might look to him as though you may not have that strong a hand, you're just trying to force him out so that you can get heads-up against the all-in player. And against an aggressive player like Hennigan, I wanted to lead at the pot.

Remember that Ma had moved all-in before the flop with short money and we both had called. Hennigan could have had an A-10 in this spot. (In fact he played an A-10 against me later on when I had pocket aces.) Or he could have had pocket nines or pocket eights, in which case he definitely would have called when I led at the pot. So, I led at the pot trying to get Hennigan to call me. I knew that I had the best hand unless he happened to have pocket sevens or tens, making it set over set between the two of us.

My thinking was "I have a big hand, I want to play

it right now." I didn't want to give off free cards on the turn and river, and then show it down on the end. I wanted to get called right away in case Hennigan had a pair.

2005 WSOP $5,000 No-Limit Hold'em
8-Handed at the Final Table
Steve Zoine, John Hennigan and Todd Brunson

Todd Brunson, who won his first WSOP bracelet later on, started this championship table in dead-last chip position. He had gone all-in several times before this hand came up, surviving each time. In one of his earlier all-in moves, he had taken a miserable beat. In that hand, Brunson went all in with the A♥ A♣ and Dustin Woolf called with the A♦ Q♣. Things were looking up for Brunson, until Lady Luck stepped in with a trick she sometimes pulls on the best hand. The final board was the 10♥ 3♠ 2♠ 5♣ 4♠. Woolf caught the miracle 4♠ on the river, elevating his dog hand to a tie when both he and Brunson made a wheel.

In this fateful hand Brunson, still short on chips, once again went all in, this time with the A♠ 3♥. John Hennigan called with the K♣ Q♣ and Steve Zoine called from the big blind with the K♦ J♥. The flop came 4♥ 2♦ J♠.

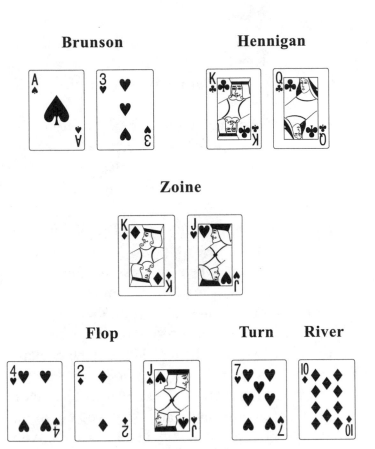

Zoine bet $25,000 with his pair of jacks, and Hennigan folded. The 7♥ came on the turn, followed by the 10♦ on the river. Brunson could not survive his final all-in hand, winning $65,705 for his eight-place finish. One week later he fared a whole lot better. Todd won the $2,500 Omaha high-low tournament for $255,945 and his first WSOP bracelet.

2005 WSOP $5,000 No-Limit Hold'em
7-Handed at the Final Table
Steve Zoine, John Hennigan and Dustin Woolf

Just after Todd Brunson went out, a three-way key hand came up that left us six-handed when it was over. At the time, Wang was still in first place with Zoine in third place behind me, Hennigan in fourth place, and Woolf in sixth.

Before the flop, Hennigan raised to $21,000 with the 4♠ 3♠. You see these types of rather mysterious raises pretty often when aggressive players like "Johnny World" are at the championship table. Usually they're trying to pick up the pot right there.

Steve Zoine called the raise with the 5♠ 5♦. Zoine got to the final table by using a strategy he explained in his interview with ESPN. "Nobody knows who I am," he said. "I'm really an unknown factor. I let the pros knock each other out, and just stayed out of their way. I folded my way to the final table." Dustin Wolfe, whose nickname in the online games he regularly wins is "Never Win," called from the blind with the A♦ 7♦.

Hennigan   Zoine

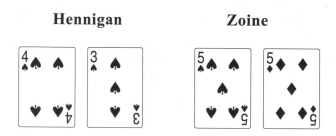

Wolfe

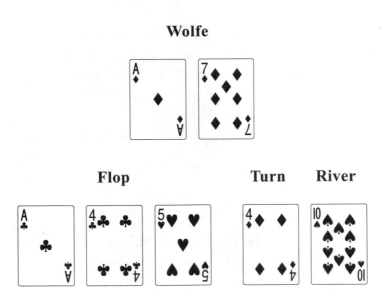

The flop came with the A♣ 4♣ 5♥. All three players caught a piece of it. Hennigan caught bottom pair with an inside-straight draw and Wolfe made top pair with a bad kicker. But it was Zoine who hit the jackpot with his set of fives. The first to act, Woolf checked, Hennigan checked behind him, and Zoine bet $40,000. Woolf called and Hennigan folded, probably figuring that his small pair was already beaten and being unwilling to make the overcall with only a gutshot straight draw.

The turn card was the 4♦. Now Woolf moved all in with two pair, aces and fours, only to get called by Zoine with his full house. The only card that could save Woolf would have been an ace on the river.

Instead the 10♠ came off the deck and Woolf went out in seventh place, taking home $87,610. Note that Johnny World saved himself a world of misery by folding on the flop. If he had decided to draw to his gutshot straight, he would have made trip fours on the turn and probably could not have gotten away from the hand. To his credit, he made the right laydown at the right time.

2005 WSOP $5,000 No-Limit Hold'em
6-Handed at the Final Table
"The Degree All-In Moment"
T.J. Cloutier versus Neal Wang

The ESPN videos of the WSOP always feature a key hand called "The Degree All-in Moment" when a player puts his tournament life on the line by pushing all his chips into the middle. In this tournament, I was that player.

The chip leader, Neal Wang, had not played many hands. I don't know whether he just wasn't catching cards or had frozen in the heat of battle. In this key hand, he brought the pot in before the flop for $30,000 with the 9♥ 9♦. I came over the top of him for $65,000 more with the A♠ Q♣. Everybody folded and Neal called the raise, making it a classic "coin-flip" situation, a pocket pair against two overcards.

The flop came with the 5♦ 2♥ 3♦. Wang checked

to me and I pushed my chips to the center, all-in. Wang called. In an apparent attempt to find out the reasoning behind my all-in move, the ESPN cameramen zeroed in on me to catch my comments. "What the hell?!" I said. "I can catch a four, an ace, or a queen to win." And then I held my breath.

The 3♣ came on the turn, making those nines look like giant killers. Then the beautiful Q♦ magically appeared on the river to save me from an early out. I doubled up and Wang was severely crippled.

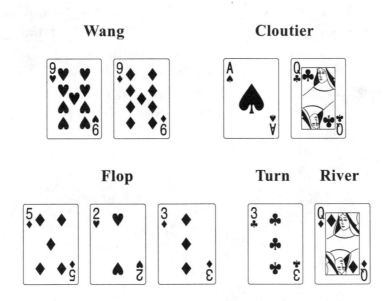

My point in discussing this hand is to emphasize that at some point in a tournament, you have to make a decision to go for it. I thought this was the right time to make a play that could take me closer to winning the championship. Luck does, after all, enter into the equation in tournament poker. Winning this hand put me in the chip lead.

2005 WSOP $5,000 No-Limit Hold'em
6-Handed at the Final Table
T.J. Cloutier versus John Hennigan

When we were six-handed, Johnny "World" Hennigan and I faced off in a $264,000 pot that sent him to the rail. Before the flop I brought it in for $20,000 with the prettiest hand in the world, the A♥ A♣. Hennigan had a pretty good hand himself, especially at a short-handed table, the A♠ 10♠. He raised all-in and I called.

Hennigan   **Cloutier**

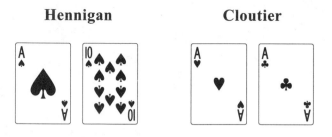

Flop			Turn	River

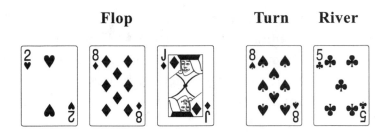

When the flop came with the 2♥ 8♦ J♦ and then the turn came with the 8♠, Hennigan stood up to leave, realizing that there was no way for him to win. By the time the 5♣ hit on the river, he was almost out the door $109,510 richer. Not bad for two days' work!

2005 WSOP $5,000 No-Limit Hold'em
5-Handed at the Final Table
John Bonetti versus Jason Berilgen

We hadn't heard much from Jason "Doc" Berilgen, a doctor from Houston who had finished twelfth in the only other big tournament he had played, a $10,000 World Poker Tour event. He had started the final table in seventh chip position and had quietly held on for most of the day, outlasting Smith, Ma, Brunson, Woolf and Hennigan.

In five-handed play, Berilgen was short-chipped. He brought it in for around $25,000 with the 6♠ 6♦, one of the best hands he'd looked at in a long time.

Unfortunately he ran into John Bonetti, who was sitting in the blind with the K♣ K♦. When Bonetti raised $25,000 more, Berilgen, already pot-committed, called all-in. "If you've got aces, I'm beat!" Bonetti said as he turned his pocket cowboys face up on the felt.

Berilgen   **Bonetti**

Flop   **Turn**   **River**

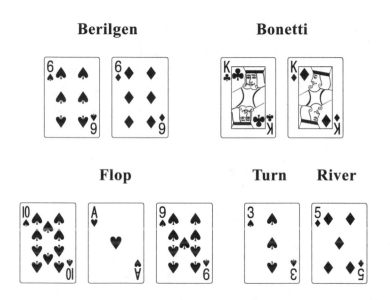

The flop came 10♠ A♥ 9♠ with the turn showing the 3♠. "Show me a spade!" the doc begged. He could only win if a six or a spade came on the river. When the 5♦ slid off the deck, the good doctor shook hands all the way around and added $131,410 to his bankroll.

We were four-handed, and Norman Chan, ESPN color commentator, couldn't resist noting that it was "two 30-somethings left against two 'Where did I leave my teeth?' somethings." Is that any way to describe a couple of senior citizens trying to eke out a living at tournament poker?!

2005 WSOP $5,000 No-Limit Hold'em
4-Handed at the Final Table
Steve Zoine versus Neal Wang

By the time this hand came up, Neal Wang, who started as the chip leader, was very low on chips. Bonetti folded under the gun and Zoine raised to $40,000 with the K♥ 5♥. Wang looked down at the K♦ 9♦ in the small blind and went all-in. I folded the K♣ 10♣, one of those trouble hands I really don't like to play, and certainly not against a raise and an all-in bet. With plenty of chips, Zoine called as the 2 to 1 underdog in the hand.

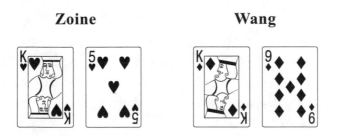

Zoine	Wang

Flop			Turn	River

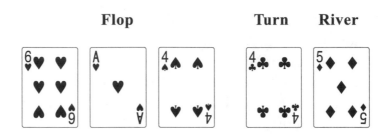

The flop came with the 6♥ A♥ 4♠ giving Zoine a flush draw. The turn card was the 4♣. Wang was still the favorite to take the pot if he could dodge a heart or a five. He couldn't. The 5♦ on the end gave Zoine the pot and sent Wang home in fourth place with a hefty $153,315 payday.

2005 WSOP $5,000 No-Limit Hold'em
3-Handed at the Final Table
T.J. Cloutier versus John Bonetti

When we got to three-handed play, John Bonetti and I played a hand that turned out to be a key hand for me. Bonetti and I had about equal chips with Steve Zoine in the lead. Holding the Q♣ Q♠, I raised the pot. Bonetti reraised with the A♣ K♥. I moved all-in and he quickly called for all his chips. The board came with the 4♠ 2♣ 2♠ J♦ 10♠. It did not improve either hand and Bonetti was eliminated in third place for a payday of $175,215.

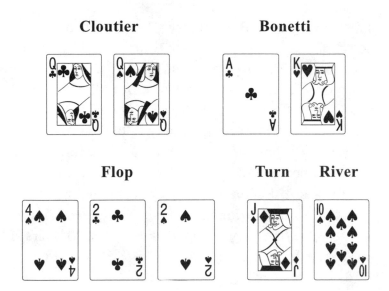

Although I have lost coin-flip situations like this many times, I still thought that moving in was the correct play because of two factors:

1. Zoine had a huge lead and I needed to win a big pot to get within double-up range of him; and
2. Pocket queens is a very good hand in three-way action and I wanted to make sure that I would get all of Bonetti's chips if I won the pot.

In an earlier confrontation with Bonetti when there were three tables left, I was in the big blind with a very substantial stack. Bonetti, who had just lost a large pot in the hand before this one, was in the small blind with about a fourth as many chips as I had. Everybody passed to Bonetti and he moved in for all his chips. I had Q-Q and called. He held a K-J, caught a king on the board, and doubled up to stay in the tournament.

Knowing how Bonetti plays after losing a big pot (whether or not he had the best hand when the hand started), I actually would have called his all-in bet with a far inferior hand than two queens. Why? Because, having played together for over 20 years, I knew that he has a tendency to move with any two cards in this scenario.

2005 WSOP $5,000 No-Limit Hold'em
Heads Up for the Championship
T.J. Cloutier versus Steve Zoine

In every tournament there seems to be a certain hand that becomes the ultimate defining hand. It doesn't have to be the final hand, just a hand that in some way will leave you with the chips and the confidence to go on and win the tournament. Such a hand occurred when Steve Zoine and I got heads-up.

This was one of the very first hands we played heads-up and at the time, Steve had a big chip lead. He raised the pot $40,000 before the flop with the 6♥ 6♠ and I just called with the J♠ 9♦. (After all, J-9 is my "name" hand!) The flop was just perfect for me. It came 7♣ 10♠ 8♠.

Zoine   Cloutier

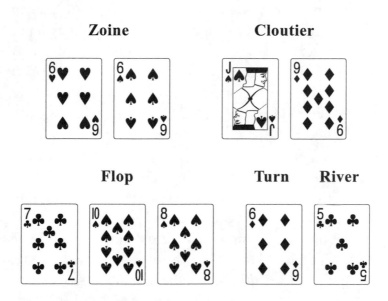

Flop   Turn   River

As soon as "my" flop hit the board, Steve decided to lead at the pot with a $40,000 bet. It looked like he wanted to play the hand, so I decided to raise an amount that I thought he would call, but not enough that my raise would scare him off the hand. I raised $100,000 more. He already had $80,000 in the pot, $40,000 before the flop and $40,000 on the flop. So $100,000 was not an unreasonable raise to try to get him to call and play with me. Essentially he only had to put in close to the same amount of money he already had in the pot. And he had a ton of chips at the time, a lot more chips than I had.

My intent was not to lose him, but to get some money in the pot and entice him to play with me. In no-limit hold'em sometimes, if you want to play a pot to the river, you want to make the kind of raise that will drag your opponent in to play with you. We call it "milking your opponent" out of his chips. Steve did not hesitate to call the raise.

The turn card—the 6♦—put him in a world of trouble. I bet $200,000 and Steve reraised another $200,000. He had trapped himself by making a very inexperienced play. I pushed the rest of my chips to the center, and Steve called with his trip sixes. Of course the board could have paired and I would have been gone. But I knew I had the nuts—and believe me, that's a great feeling! When the harmless 5♣ came on the river, I dragged in the monster pot and took the lead away from Steve.

This pot should never have become as large as it became—and it wouldn't have if Steve hadn't made a major mistake when he called my raise on the flop. There was nothing wrong with his leading at the pot on the flop; he was trying to win it right there. But once I raised him $100,000 more, he was supposed to deck his hand right then. He only had an under pair to the board, with an inside draw to the ignorant end of the straight, so there were a lot of possible hands that could beat him. As a result of winning this huge pot, I doubled up to take over the lead in chips, and dictated the action that followed.

2005 WSOP $5,000 No-Limit Hold'em
The Final Hand at the Championship Table
T.J. Cloutier versus Steve Zoine

When the final hand of the tournament was dealt, I had three-fourths of the chips. Zoine raised $50,000 with the A♥ K♠ and I reraised $250,000 more with the A♦ 5♥. Steve pushed in the rest of his chips, and I called. Heads-up with a 3-1 lead, my thinking was that an A-5 looked like a pretty good hand, but of course Steve's hand was a big favorite.

Being out-chipped by 3 to 1, Zoine was in a desperate mood. When he raised, I reraised enough to essentially put him all in if he called. He could've had jack-high, ten-high, queen-high or king-high, in which case I would've had the best hand with ace-high. As it turned out, of course, he had the best hand with an A-K.

Cloutier	Zoine

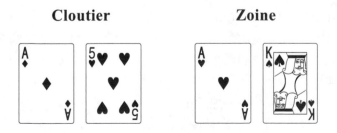

Flop   **Turn**   **River**

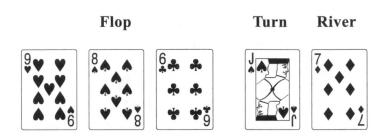

When we turned our hands over, the TV crew recorded my words: "I'm ready to draw out for once," I said. And I did just that when I made a gutshot straight on the river to win the final hand and the championship.

In an earlier pot that came up four hands before the end of the tournament, I had an 8 to 1 chip lead over Steve. I picked up two kings and he held an A-7 offsuit. We got all of Steve's money in before the flop. An ace came on the board and Steve doubled up to about one-fourth of the chips to get back into the ballgame. I am mentioning this K-K versus A-7 hand because, in the television coverage of our final play, they didn't explain that this hand had come up previously.

Because of that omission, my play with the A-5 in our final hand might've looked like the dumbest play in the world when it actually wasn't a bad play at all. I would not have played the A-5 as aggressively as I did if I hadn't had a big chip lead. But since I had my opponent on the ropes, I thought the timing was correct. Even if I had lost the hand, I still would've had at least half the chips. After all, Columbus took a chance!

At the end of the tournament, we shook hands. "You played great, buddy," I said to Steve.

"Thanks, I appreciate that, I appreciate it a lot," he answered. "I read your book and I think it improved my game tremendously."

"Zoine read TJ's book but got beat by the author," the TV announcer said. Steve was referring to *Championship No-Limit & Pot-Limit Hold'em*, which I wrote with Tom McEvoy.

"If I had to pick someone at the final table," Zoine said in his exit interview, "T.J. would've been the last one I would've picked to play heads up with. But what more could I ask for? The whole experience was unbelievable!"

"Zoine is gracious in defeat," the announcer said.

I couldn't agree more. I just wish the players at every championship table conducted themselves with the good manners and respect for our opponents that we all displayed in this tournament. Zoine collected $352,620 for his fine play at the championship table. I won $657,100 and my sixth bracelet.

PART 10

More Tournament Strategies

WHEN YOU HIT THAT STONE WALL IN TOURNAMENTS

"When I get to a certain point in the tournament, I fade. What can I do?" A lot of online players have told me that when they get to a certain level in the tournament, they seem to hit a stone wall. They start in a tournament with 700 players, for example, and when it gets down to 150 players, they bomb. Sometimes they don't give me all the facts, but in most cases they had enough money to last a while longer. But when they hit the higher blinds, they were so short stacked they couldn't get past them.

If you get to a certain spot and hit that stone wall, you'd better take a look at what you have been doing at that level. Maybe you did something you shouldn't have done; indeed, at some point, it's highly likely that you did something wrong. Maybe it wasn't just bad luck that you got knocked out.

Ask yourself, "What quality of hands have I been playing?" When you're playing online, bring up the history of the hands you've played. Looking at your hand history, you can determine whether you were playing too loose or too tight or just plain bad. Or in a live tournament, you might write down every hand you play. When you get knocked out of a tournament, you should be able to remember your last 10 hands at the least. Sure, you're going to get drawn out on occasionally, but that's just part of the game.

I know people who have played real well for three days in a four-day tournament. Then they get dealt pocket kings and push their chips into the middle. Somebody takes a flyer against them with an A-10 or A-J, pops an ace on the board, and takes them out. You can't help it when those things happen. But that won't happen all the time.

When you're running bad—and everybody who's ever played poker has unlucky streaks—you play bad too. It's a combination of both. I've caught myself doing it. If I'm running bad, I'll sometimes make errors that a schoolboy wouldn't make. You start taking chances to make up for the chips you've lost. Then you get in a hurry and start putting more gamble into your play when you know you shouldn't. If you're a good player, you know that if you just let the natural run of cards come, you're going to get the money over a period of time.

That's just the way it is—the better players are going to get the money. It might take a very long time for the percentages to catch up with you and do what they're supposed to do for you, but sooner or later, everybody supposedly holds the same amount of good cards.

Another reason you might hit a stone wall when you get deep into a tournament that started with a lot of players is that the players you were beating up on to stay alive were bad players. Now most of them are gone. Some of them are still in there with chips because they've been lucky, but once 550 players are gone from a field of 700, most of the players still in action can play poker. At least they have a semblance of being good players, certainly a lot better than the original crew.

This means that you have to play better too. You can't make any mistakes. Get crazy and you're gone. Just because you won a pot when you raised with an A-J from around back and the blind called you with a weaker ace doesn't mean that play is going to work for you later on.

Whether you're playing online or in a casino, you can see what your opponents are doing, how they're playing, and what they're winning with—and who's playing a lot of pots and who isn't. You have to adjust your play to their play, and to the constantly changing circumstances in tournaments. Review the hands you've played, look at the position from which you played them, analyze your actions, and make a plan to correct your mistakes. That way, instead of butting your head against that stone wall, you should be able to break through it on your way to the top.

ON OUTTHINKING YOURSELF IN TOURNAMENTS

A lot of people outthink themselves in poker tournaments and make mistakes as the consequence. For example, suppose the blinds are coming to a player I'll call Joe. You know that Joe can't stand to go through the blinds again because, if he does, he'll have so short a stack, he won't have any chance at all. So you figure that he's going to play a marginal hand, and he'll probably bring it in for his whole stack. You've noticed that players do it all the time in tournaments.

Say that you're playing seven-handed and you're sitting in the fifth seat. Sure enough, Joe has moved all in and nobody has called him yet. "I'm gonna call this guy with my Q-J," you think. "There's a pretty good chance I have the best hand in this spot. I know Joe's moving in because he's gonna have to put up the big blind in the next hand." You have decided to play policeman. But you've forgotten one little thing—two players are sitting behind you. You call him with your marginal cards, and get raised from behind. Or you call him and find out the hard way that Joe actually has a hand. Either way, you get knocked off.

And either way, you didn't have to give up those chips. And certainly, you didn't have to play policeman to start with. If I had called him, I would've made sure that I was in a position where I couldn't get rehashed. And although I might have called him with a marginal hand, it wouldn't have been a queen-high hand. I would had at least a king with another paint or a K-10. And I would have had a lot of chips so that my call wouldn't hurt me too much if I lost the pot. See the difference in the situation?

To automatically play policeman because you've figured out that your opponent had to move in, you'd better have a little something. Short-stacked players don't always play desperate hands. I've seen players like John Inashima and Tony Cousineau hang on forever when they're short stacked. But when they finally put their money in, they usually have a decent hand. You certainly don't want to be playing policeman when there are 150 players still in the tournament. Your object is not to knock people out, it is to build your stack and stay alive.

A lot of players make this type of mistake at the final table. They try to arrest the felon and end up in handcuffs and shackles—and wonder how they got there! They start with a decent stack but their stack starts dwindling because they figure they have to be the one who catches the short stack that's making a move, or the aggressive guy who's out of line. They make bad, bad moves when they didn't have to. Then they get short-stacked, pick up two queens, get them beat by somebody with an A-8, and they're out of the tournament. And that's the only thing they remember, the *only* thing. They forget all the hands they played badly before they were dealt the two queens. They forget the mistakes they made that caused them to become so short-chipped that they didn't have enough money to blow the other guy out of the pot.

It's like a snowball rolling down hill. If I make a bad play, I know I'm pretty much gone. Anybody who's played poker for as many years as I have knows when he's made a bad play. I don't know if you do it, but I get so stone-headed sometimes. I'll say to myself, "Now, this guy's running good and that guy's running good. Stay clear of them." So, who are the two guys I play pots against? Those two! Go figure. If they're running so damned good, why would I want to help them?!

THE BIGGEST MISTAKE AMATEURS MAKE IN NO-LIMIT HOLD'EM

In the first chapter of this book, I discussed the things that separate great poker players from average players. At the top of my list is the premise that great players make fewer mistakes than anybody else. Further, top players know they're making a mistake while they're doing it, not after it's done. Amateurs play hands they shouldn't play and they don't know they're making a mistake.

Most of the mistakes that amateurs make in no-limit hold'em are made with hands that they call raises with. I repeat, by calling raises with hands they shouldn't call with. Here's a scenario that came to me from "Joe," a great split-pot player who has just started playing no-limit poker. He had just busted out of a big tournament in about 50th place, and told me about the hand that sent him to the rail. The man right in front of the button raised to $5,400. Joe was in the big blind with the K♣ J♣ and already had $1,600 in the pot from posting the big blind. He was kinda low on chips with about $34,000 left in his stack. He called the raise. The flop came Q♣ 10♣ 4♦. They got it all in. His opponent had pocket queens and Joe lost the hand when he didn't hit a flush or a straight.

"You only made one mistake on the hand," I told him.

"What was that?" he asked. "I flopped a draw to a royal flush!"

"It definitely wasn't your play after the flop—it was your play before the flop," I replied. "You're not supposed to call a raise with the hand. When you get hands like K-Q, K-J, K-10, Q-J, Q-10, remember that they're all trap hands. And invariably, whenever you call a raise with them and get a flop to them, you get broke to them."

"You mean, I've got $1,600 in the pot and I call $3,800 more and that's a mistake?!" he asked.

"If you're calling, knowing that you probably have the worst hand, that's a mistake," I answered. "And more people make that mistake than any other mistake in no-limit hold'em."

When people ask, "How do you survive so long all

the time?" part of my answer is that I'm not going to make the mistake Joe made. I'm not saying that I won't go up and over somebody with that hand. I might even go over the top of them with a 7-2, but I do it because I've put them on a bad hand, not two queens. But do I call a bet with a trouble hand?

No. Invariably you either get some kind of flop to it and lose your chips, or you don't flop at all to it and have to throw the hand away losing the chips you called with. Joe was out of position; he had to act first after the flop. And with that kind of flop, he was gonna play the hand no matter what. He was a dog to just about anything before the flop. If the guy had raised with an A-K, he was a dog; if he had raised with an A-4, he was still a dog. He was a dog to any kind of hand unless the raiser had something like two tens, in which case he would be in a coin-flip situation. Even then, he's still an underdog. Or suppose the guy had raised with an A-J and a jack flopped. Again Joe is gonna get broke to the hand.

Compare your plusses to your minuses with these trap hands, and you don't get many plusses. Most of the time you're not going to flop to it anyway, so you've gotta check. And you can't call any kind of a bet. If you decide to bluff at the pot and run into a better hand, you're gonna lose that money. The plusses just aren't there.

Dana Smith, my editor, told me that in her interviews with more than 100 top poker players, most of the bad beat stories they told her started with "I was in the blind." That's because the majority of mistakes are made when players call raises from the blinds with hands they shouldn't call with. Once you put your blind money in the pot, it doesn't belong to you, it belongs to the pot. If you have the mindset that it's not your money any longer, that's a good way to think.

Here's another losing scenario in tournaments, one that doesn't involve calling a raise. See if you can answer this question: In no-limit hold'em, what is the tournament situation where more money is lost than in any other? The answer is: the big blind in an unraised pot when you flop the bottom two pair. If you're up against an opponent who has flopped top pair, the bottom two pair are not protected. A lot of times, the player who has top pair will make another pair to go with it after all the money goes in and beat your two bottom two pair. It's possible that more big pots are lost in that situation than in any other in no-limit hold'em.

As Tom McEvoy, my writing partner for *Championship No-Limit & Pot-Limit Hold'em,* would say in closing, "I hope to meet you in the winners circle one day soon." Provided that we don't waste our chips by calling raises with the wrong kinds of hands, or losing a huge pot with bottom two pair.

ON GATHERING CHIPS AT THE START OF A TOURNAMENT

How do certain players accumulate chips at the start of a tournament? I am often asked that question. I don't have the definitive answer, but I think it has a lot to do with taking more chances in the early stages, and getting lucky when it counts the most. Of course we tend to notice all the times when they get a lot of chips early, but we don't take into account all the times that they're knocked out early.

There's no doubt that players who play a particular style will get the chips if they get lucky on their early gambles. They play real fast, and they play a lot of draws. I've seen a few of them get high and play any two cards and just win, win, win with them, but in the long run, they lose their chips. How many times have you noticed that the chip leader on day one didn't make it to the final table?

If that's the style of tournament poker you want to play, then play that way. But as for me, I'm going to stick to my own style. I will adjust it to a particular player, but I won't adjust it overall. When I start a tournament, I'm going to play my style because over the years I've found that if I don't, I'm out quickly. And that's a big reason why I stick with what has worked for me over the years. As we say in Texas, "If it ain't broke, don't fix it."

A BIG SLICK STORY

In our first book on how to win at no-limit and pot-limit hold'em, Tom McEvoy and I wrote in depth about how to play A-K. Not wanting to repeat myself more than I already have in this book, I decided not to go into that topic in any great detail this time around. But I couldn't resist including this big-slick story that Don Vines, co-author with Tom McEvoy of *How to Win No-Limit Hold'em Tournaments*, brought to me. This is our exact conversation.

"I was playing a tournament at the Bellagio," Don started off. "Five players were in the pot and I had A-K in the small blind. I moved in. That was the stupidest play I've ever made."

"To move in might've been," I said, "but raising wasn't a bad play."

"I repeat, stupidest play I've ever made. Why? Because I didn't think before I acted. I should've asked myself: What could be out there against me? What are they limping with? I know that somebody is limping with an ace, somebody must be limping with a king, so how much of the flop am I going to get?"

"You're right. So what happened next?"

"Everybody folds except the guy on the button, who has a pair of fives. It's his first tournament and he doesn't know he's supposed to fold. And he broke me. Correction: I got broke because it was an idiot play on my part."

"Why did you move in with A-K instead of just raising?"

"Because I didn't have that many chips, I was pretty short, and I would've been pot-committed anyway if I had just raised."

"Oh, you couldn't just raise? Well, I don't think that's the worst mistake I've ever heard. There was a chance that you might've picked up all five of their bets. It wasn't as though you were going all in with an A-5, you were doing it was an A-K. That's a pretty big hand in no-limit hold'em."

I ended our conversation by mentioning once again that the hand that players lose the most money with in no-limit hold'em tournaments is the A-K. If you reviewed my career and you found out how many times I went out of a tournament with A-K, you'd be absolutely flabbergasted. And a lot of times it was when I was up against an ace with a smaller kicker. But it's a hand that you *should* play in a lot of situations, so you play it. Like I've said before, though, big slick can get a little slippery.

ON OBSERVATION

In another conversation with Don, we talked about how to improve your observation skills in tournaments. His wife and my editor, Dana Smith, set up the discussion for us by starting off with, "In your first classic on no-limit play, we got some feedback from players who said, 'TJ says that he would notice if a wing dropped off a gnat at the other end of the table, and that he has a photographic memory. Sure it's easy for people like that to have good instincts, but do you have to have TJ's huge observation skills and a photographic memory to become a top notch poker player?'"

My answer to that is no. You can't develop a photographic memory, but anybody can develop observations skills, that part is for sure. When you play in a game, if you really want to improve, you should be able to remember three or four key hands and how they were played. And that's enough. If you have to write them down when you go home at night to remember them, do it.

"When you get to a table and you see the players," Don added, "you want to see whether the ones you know are doing the same things wrong that they've always done wrong. For example, I know a player who gets married to a king. It doesn't matter what the kicker is, if he has a king, he plays it. And he's not alone: a lot of other no-limit players play K-Q like they had pocket aces. And you'd also better study the other ones in a hurry to find out what they're doing that day."

Let me add that people who work at different day jobs and want to climb the corporate ladder keep trying to learn ways to do their job better all the time. Playing poker is a job. And if you want to get good at it, you try to learn something every time you play.

A big part of your learning curve involves improving your observation skills.

As big as poker has become, it's a pretty good profession to be in right now. Sure, it can be a very expensive occupation, but it's well worth the effort it takes to become a better player. There's a lot of money to be made in poker these days, and improving your observation skills will help you win your slice of the poker pie.

THE DUMBEST PLAY I'VE EVER MADE

I've told you some stories about players making bad plays. Now let me tell you about the dumbest play I've ever made. It happened at the $25,000 tournament at the Bellagio a few years ago. I still think I should've taken home the $2.7 million, but I didn't. And there's a good reason why!

My opponent in this hand had raised 10 out of the previous 13 pots. Now he raises the eleventh out of fourteen pots in a row. I was on the button, so I called him with a 9-8 suited. There were four of us who had over two million in chips at the time and I had $2.3 million. When I called his raise, I immediately formulated my plan. "If I don't flop to this 9-8 (a good flop like two pair, or trip eights or nines), I hope an ace comes off because I'll take this pot away from him," I decided.

Well, the flop came A-J-4. He made a little baby bet and I moved him in for $1,700,000, exactly what he had in front of him. Guess what? He had two aces in the hole and called me in a New York minute. I've made the same play lots of times, so I can't really fault myself, but it was a helluva time to do it. Sometimes you get what you wish for, right? I wasn't even supposed to call his first raise, which was only about $80,000, but I still could've gotten away from the hand on the flop. Instead I lost $1,700,000 to it. Sometimes a so-called great player's timing might not be perfect!

PART 11

More Thoughts from T.J.

TOURNAMENTS HAVE CHANGED

I see stuff happening these days in tournaments that I never used to see. It's something like the major league baseball teams. You'll notice that the ERA in pitching has risen way up. There are just so many pitchers to go around, and they have to fill the roster and have pitchers pitch so that the ERA has gone way up from what it used to be. And that has happened because of the saturation of teams. There are so many more teams now, and so they need more players. And they don't get quite the quality they used to get.

It's the same in poker. We're getting more and more players, so that a lot of times early in the tournament, the quality of the play is nowhere near as good as it used to be. There are more draw-outs, obviously. When we were playing with 100 players versus 500 players, the difference in the types of hands being played is enormous, because of the number of players in the field and their general lack of experience.

When you see these huge fields with a lot of players in them who are inexperienced, the variety of hands played in the early rounds is much broader than when the fields were smaller in general. You can sit at a table and see players winning pots and getting a lot of chips early, knowing that they were lucky to win them. But you also know in your mind that they're not going to be there late in the tournament because, as the tournament field shrinks, as the tables condense, you will be facing better players than you were facing to start with.

You might start at a table where you're playing against one or two or three good players, and six players who are average, who are decent players but not good players. Later on in the tournament, things might be just the opposite: there might be three who aren't so good and six who are good. You might not see all the good players survive to the end, because a lot of times weaker players will make it, but usually for only that one time in their careers. But at the least, there will be a sprinkling of good players at the end. When a weak player makes it, he comes back next time, thinking that maybe the cards will run over him again, but they just might not. And if they don't, he has no chance.

More and more, the players who are winning the big tournaments are people that have been very successful in other things. They are very smart people. Howard Lederer is very intelligent, Gus Hansen is probably the top backgammon player in the world, and Chris Ferguson has a Ph.D. in game theory. They're people who can think, who understand the theory, and can execute when the time is right. I like what Paul Phillips said in a column he wrote for MSNBC: "What separates good players is not knowledge but execution." And that's what today's highly educated tournament players do best, no matter how big the fields or how tough the competition.

ON MAKING DEALS

I'm not into making deals, but a lot of people are. I am not anti-deal, it's just that if you're going to make a deal with me, you're not going to like it. I'm going to get the best of it at all times. And I say that up front. You're not going to like the deal that I propose.

There are so many little nuances that occur in poker. Here's a story from an ace-to-five lowball tournament. I played a guy head-up years ago at Amarillo Slim's tournament at the High Sierra in Lake Tahoe. When he looked at his cards, it was absolutely pure that whatever he had to draw, he took out of his hand and set it aside. I knew how many cards he was drawing every single time. There's no way in the world this man is supposed to be able to beat me, I thought. When we got head-up, we were playing $20,000-$40,000 limits at that time and we were fairly equal in chips. "Do you want to do any business?" he asked me. "No, I don't think so," I answered.

On the very first hand we were dealt head-up, I looked down at A-2-3-4-4, a fantastic lowball hand.

Looking over at him, I saw that he had two cards sitting over to the side so I knew that he was going to draw two cards. He raised and I reraised and he called. He drew his two and I drew my one. I paired my deuce and he made an 8-5 low to win the pot. Now he had about $100,000 more chips than I had. "Will you make a deal now?" he asked. "Well, I'll chop it with you," I answered. "You got it!" he said, in a New York minute.

Even though I always knew how many cards he was drawing, I said to myself, "If I can't win this pot, I'm not gonna beat this guy, so I might as well get half the money." As it turned out, that was the first tournament he'd ever played.

IS IT TOUGHER TO WIN TOURNAMENTS TODAY?

I don't agree with commentators who say that it's getting tougher and tougher to win tournaments these days because of all the loose players who get lucky early on. Fifteen years ago we had the same complaints about players making loose moves. We had A-K and somebody with Q-10 beat us. It's nothing new. Everything you see from these new players you've seen before. You just see more of it today because all the tournaments are so much bigger, that's all. And so you have to overcome it more often than you used to.

I've taken beats all my life, but I've put beats on people all my life too. It's all a part of the game. The only difference is the numbers—the game itself has not changed one iota. More people are taking chances, it's true, because of the greater number of players. And we have the satellite system, in part, to thank for today's huge fields. A fellow who had won a $250 satellite was playing the first day of the WSOP. He suspected he had the weakest hand before the flop when a top player came over the top of him.

"What the heck," he said. "It only cost me $250 to play," and he shoved his chips into the pot. And he beat the good player. This is an example of people taking more risks in today's tournaments.

Billy Baxter told me the story of how he went out on the first day of the Series. "Some guy raised before the flop with a 6-4 and I moved him all in with Big Slick," Billy said. 'I've come to gamble!' the young man said and called my reraise. He won and here I am talking to you." These things are going to happen, but I saw them happen years ago too, just not as often.

I may be in the minority when I say that the game hasn't changed, but I truly believe that. It is only the number of players that has changed, and the number of people who don't know any better. That's the key. Phil Hellmuth has a point when he laments all the bad beats that good players take at the hands of beginners. But I wish he wouldn't act the way he does on TV. We've jokingly suggested to Phil, "Why don't you put that speech on tape so you won't have to move your lips next time?"

What's happened to poker that I don't like is this: it has made a lot of bad winners, not bad losers, who jump up and down and yell "Yeah, baby, I won that one!" while the tournament is going on. In the old days you never said anything to players when you beat them. Why would you rub salt in their wounds? Now they're doing it even before the TV cameras arrive. They get so far out of line. And as soon as somebody gets broke, some players don't even give them a chance to leave their seats before yelling, "Seat open, seat open!" Imagine how terrible the loser feels—he's just lost his money and now he's getting the hustle out of his seat.

I've even heard veteran players say, "If it wasn't for loose players like you, I could've won this tournament." But if it wasn't for players like that, they might not win any tournaments! Just remember that when the skill levels are equal and every player starts with the same number of chips, it is the player who gets lucky who wins.

IT'S ABOUT TIME TO BURY DEAD MONEY

We're seeing a lot of final tables in tournaments these days where several of the finalists have played online poker only and are playing their first brick-and-mortar casino tournament. Today it's not unusual for one-half of them to be faces you've never seen in the poker world. To a lot of people, it might appear to be a fluke that they're at the championship table fighting for the title against well-known players.

In the old days when there were fewer than 200 players entering the main event at the *World Series of Poker*—in 1985 when I came second to Bill Smith there were 140 entries—we all used to remark that there was more "dead money" in the $10,000 tournament than in any other event. We meant that they had practically no chance of winning, and that's how the expression "dead money" got started. But if you still believe there's that much dead money in today's big tournaments, you're dead wrong. In the old days you could bet on a core of 25 to 50 players to win the Big One. These days you could pick the top 150 players and give somebody else the field—and the field would be a big favorite.

With all the poker books, poker seminars, and opportunities to practice online these days, there is no longer any room for the dead-money concept in poker tournaments. Today everybody can play on a certain level, though obviously some players, the so-called pros, are better than others. What the pros sometimes forget is that anyone with some basic knowledge of how to play the game can pick up a hand here, a hand there, and suddenly have a whole lot of chips. And on any given day, a lot of chips combined with some old-fashioned horse sense, can lead you to the winners' circle regardless of your level of experience.

Should you adjust your play according to the

experience of the players you're up against? That's the question. I'm not sure you should adjust it to their level of experience, but you certainly must adjust your play according to how they're playing right now, what you've seen them do, and how you visualize their probable play. A lot of these young players are pretty well experienced through playing on the Internet. Their problem is that now they have to look at you eye-to-eye. A lot of them play multiple tournaments online and have developed a lot of skill in how to play, but it's a little bit different when you have to look your opponents in the eye, knowing that they're looking you in the eye too.

A lot of people have asked me whether it's easier or tougher to play against inexperienced players. I admit that it's nice when I get to a final table and I already know how everybody plays—the way it was in the old days—because then I don't have to figure it out. But I also like going to a table that has three or four players I haven't played with before and having to figure out how they play. It's a challenge that I enjoy.

Isn't it more likely that a pro will take a bad beat at a table like that? I've been asked that question a lot. Yes, it is. But playing against people you don't know keeps you alert because you have to learn how they're playing. Instead of just sitting down, relaxing and getting into your comfort zone against a bunch of players you already know, your juices start flowing, you're on your toes learning how they play.

Once I learn what they're doing, I'll never forget it, so the next time we play together I'll remember them. I certainly don't think of them as dead money, which brings me back to my major point.

The commentary at the 2003 *World Series of Poker* aggravated me because I thought the announcers were out of line by putting so much emphasis on dead money. They showed a picture of Bob and Maureen Feduniak and referred to them as being dead money. What?! She had just finished fourth on a Party Poker cruise tournament, and had beaten Howard Lederer heads-up in a Bellagio tournament. And of course, Bob is well known as a successful tournament player. I just didn't appreciate it. No matter who it is, I believe that labeling people dead money is bad for poker. What about this businessman who wants to play? "I know I don't have much chance of winning, but do I want everybody in the world to think that I'm a fool, that I'm just giving my $10,000 away?" he asks himself. Shouldn't we be encouraging people to play poker instead of driving them away?

Chris Moneymaker was ballyhooed as dead money throughout the opening segments of the 2003 *WSOP* coverage. He set that notion to rest. It's about time we bury it forever.

JUST A TOUCH MORE MODESTY, PLEASE

The e-mails I receive from online players usually start off with, "I'm a pretty good player, but ..." Then they say they need a little help here and there on some phase of their tournament strategy, like how to bet the right amount or when to go all in. But invariably, they tell me up front that they are very good players. And that makes me wonder how they have set their criteria for good players.

When I get these e-mails, I'd rather hear the writer say, "I think I play okay, but I need a little help here and there." But to tell me how great they are, no. Or to tell me that there's no use in their playing a certain game online, or playing their home game, because the players are so weak just doesn't cut it. It leaves me wondering, "If you're that good, why haven't I heard of you before? And why are you asking me for help?"

When you're playing in low-limit games online or in your home game, you usually are not playing against people who are trying to make a living at poker. They're playing for fun, so they're not going to play as well as some of the players you're going to face in major tournaments, players who have the skill to seize so many situations against you.

When you step out of your comfort zone and step up to a major tournament in Vegas or California or Foxwoods where you're playing against top players, it's a huge leap. The players you play against in the big events are tried and tested. I wrote something about getting your slice of the pie in one of my previous books. In it, I mentioned that there are only so many pieces of the pie available to each player, if any at all. If you're the local champion, I think you should try playing a major tournament against other local champs and players who are well known to see how well you play against stiffer competition. Maybe you'll get your slice of the pie.

But if you don't cut out a slice for yourself, if you don't do well, I suggest that you go back and play in the game you've been beating, where things were a lot easier for you than when you ventured out on the road. I think you should try it, but I don't think you should be spouting off about how good you are until you've done something.

When I say you've done something, I mean you've played against some top players and actually proved what you can do. You don't necessarily have to do it in tournaments, you can do it in live games. Or go out to the different spots in the country where you know they have very good games and top players. If it's no-limit hold'em you're looking for, there are big cash games all over California these days. See how you do in those.

When you move into playing some big tournaments, of course, you have to know how to adjust your play with correct tournament strategy because the blinds are raised continually. But you're not necessarily going to be "dead money," even in the first major tournament you enter. I just don't believe in dead money. To me, dead money is someone who buys into a $10,000 championship event so that everybody at work or at the company he owns can see that he played in the big one. He plays one or two hands, gets an A-2, and moves in with it. Now, that is dead money. But you see very little of that these days.

When we had 100 players in the big one at the WSOP, people used to say, "There's 100 players here and 50 of them have no chance. They're dead money." The 50 dead-money players they identified were people who had walked in off the street and had hardly ever played poker. Those days are gone. Today's players are very experienced. Just because they are online players who haven't played face to face with other people doesn't mean that they can't play in a live tournament. It simply means that they have to learn how to do it.

If you're one of the thousands of online players who want to learn how to win a live tournament, you've picked up the right book. But when you e-mail me or another seasoned tournament champion for advice, you might want to approach the improvement of your game with a touch more modesty.

BAD BEATS AND LAME LAMENTS

The lamest thing that I hear players say in no-limit hold'em is, "I got aces beat." Unless you have the opportunity to get all in before the flop with pocket aces, you should never complain about getting aces cracked. Why? Because all you got beat was one pair. That's right, one pair! There are a zillion hands that beat one pair in hold'em. So, if you get beaten with them, you have no story to tell. You simply got one pair beat. Any two pair, any three of a kind, any straight, any flush beat two aces.

The only time it's a really bad beat is when you get all your money in before the flop in a tournament, and then you get beat when you started with the best hand by far. Unless that's what happened, you can throw your aces-cracked, bad-beat story in the trashcan where it belongs.

PART 12

TJ's Top Tips for Playing No-Limit Hold'em

EIGHT TIPS FROM T.J.

TIP 1
PLAY YOUR OPPONENTS
Learn as much as you can as soon as you can about your opponents. Then play their individual strengths and weaknesses against them.

TIP 2
PLAY YOUR POSITION
Be aware of your position in every hand you play. When you are the last to act, use your superior position to your benefit. When you are in an early position, only play very strong hands because you are out of position.

TIP 3
PLAY THE SITUATION
Size up the situation in each pot you play. If it looks favorable to you, play your hand in a way that will give you the advantage over your opponent(s).

TIP 4
PLAY THE RIGHT CARDS

Be smart with the types of cards you start a hand with. Only play good starting hands in proper position. Always try to avoid playing trap hands.

TIP 5
PLAY THE RIGHT CHIPS

When you have the right read on an opponent, and decided on the right play, you also need to make the right bet. If you want him to play with you, try to bet an amount that you believe he will call. If you want to close him out of the pot, bet an amount that you think he cannot possibly call.

TIP 6
PLAY IN CONTROL

When you're in a heads-up situation, always try to dictate all of the action. Make a conscious effort to never let your opponent have the upper hand. This is especially important when you have the lead in chips.

TIP 7
PLAY WITH A PLAN

Always prepare your game plan in advance. Have an idea of which opponents you are going to attack and the ones you are going to give a wide path to. Having a game plan can give you confidence, but be willing to alter your plan if things change and it isn't working for you.

TIP 8
PLAY TO WIN

Always have winning the tournament be your ultimate goal. Even though you may make a nice payday, never be truly satisfied with less than first place. If you expect to win, you will be motivated to play your best poker.

PART 13

Glossary of Poker Terms

All in. Betting all the chips or cash you have left in your stack. "When T.J. raised, I went *all in* with pocket kings. Unfortunately, he called my *all-in* bet with pocket aces and sent me to the rail."

Add on. The final rebuy that you can make at the end of the rebuy period in rebuy tournaments. "I only *add on* when I think that it will make my stack more competitive."

Behind you (sitting). Any player who can act after you do. "Jack decided not raise with his pocket jacks because he was afraid that Brad, who was *sitting behind* him, might reraise and put him all in."

Bluff. Betting with an inferior hand in the hope of stealing the pot. "The cowboy's *bluff* with nothing-cards drove Alto out of the pot at the championship table in 1984."

Bully. Play aggressively (particularly in hold'em) in an attempt to get your opponent(s) to fold what may be the best hand. "My opponents weren't going to be easily *bullied,* so I didn't want to do a lot of aggressive raising."

Buy-in. The amount of money it costs you to enter a tournament. Usually, the larger the buy-in, the tougher the competition. "I wanted to *buy into* the championship event, but the *buy-in* was about $9,000 more than I could afford."

Case chips. Your last chips. "It took my *case chips* to call Sexton's raise on the river."

Case (ace). The last card of that rank in the deck. "When the *case ace* came on the river, Dana made a full house to beat Tom's nut flush."

Change gears. Change your style of play from aggressive to passive, from tight to loose, from fast to slow, and so on. "I had to slow down and *change gears* in order to survive the late stage of the Four Queens Classic championship event."

Check. Although you don't make a bet, you're still able to hold your cards. Then if someone sitting behind you bets, you must either call the bet, raise, or fold your cards. "When everybody *checked* the flop to Amir, he raised with a 7-6 offsuit. They all folded, and he scooped in the pot."

Check-raise. You check with a good hand in the hope of raising if someone bets. "After the flop, Daniel checked to Jeff, who made a modest bet. Daniel then *check-raised* him with pocket aces."

Chip status. A comparison of the amount of chips you have in relation to how many chips your opponents have. "At the start of the 2000 World Series of Poker championship table, T.J. was dead last in *chip status*. He moved up four spot to finish second to Chris Ferguson."

Cold call. Call a raise without having already put the initial bet into the pot. "When Jack *cold called* after Tuna raised and Brad reraised, they knew they were in trouble."

Come over the top of. Raise or reraise an opponent's bet. "Are your opponents more liberal and therefore more likely to *come over the top* of you with a raise?"

Commit. Put in as many chips as necessary to play your hand to the river, even if they are your case chips. "If I think the odds are in my favor, I will *fully commit.*"

Dog. Poker slang meaning that your hand is the underdog. "When I looked at Catherine's two kings at the showdown, I knew that my 10-9 offsuit was a big *dog.*"

Double through. Going all-in against an opponent in order to double your stack if you win the hand. "I was so low on chips, I knew I had to *double through* somebody to build up my stack."

Flat call. Call an opponent's bet rather than raising. "Playing somewhat less aggressively than I perhaps should have, I just *flat called* the raise."

Get away from your hand. Fold, usually what appears to be a premium hand until an unfavorable flop negates its potential. "It's easy *to get away from* pocket kings when the flops comes with an ace."

Get the right price. The pot odds are favorable enough for you to justify calling a bet or a raise with a drawing hand. "You can generally defend the big blind with any pocket pair because you will usually be getting *the right price*."

Get full value. Betting, raising, and reraising in order to manipulate the size of the pot so that you will be getting maximum pot odds if you win the hand. "After raising on every round, I was able to *get full value* when my hand held up on the river."

Get there. Make your hand. "What happens when you don't *get there*, when you miss your hand? You cry a little."

Give action. Betting, calling, raising, or reraising. "Be cautious about *giving too much action* if your kicker is weak."

Give up your hand. Fold. "I *gave up my hand* when he raised."

Gutshot. The card that completes an inside-straight draw. If you hold a 9-8 and the board is showing 10-6-2, you need a 7 to complete your straight. "In the small blind, I was all in with a 9-8. On the 10-6-2 flop, I had a *gutshot* draw at a straight. The seven on the river made my day!"

In the dark. You do not peek at your hole cards. "Tuna was so low on chips when he bet, Jack called him *in the dark*."

Ignorant end. The low end of a straight. If you have a 6-5 in your hand and the board cards are showing 9-8-7, you have the lower of two possible straights. The common axiom in poker is to avoid drawing to a lower straight when a higher one also is possible. "I got punished by a higher straight when I drew to the *ignorant end* of it. Then I kicked myself for making such an elementary blunder."

Key Card. The one card that will make your hand. "I knew I needed to catch a deuce, the *key card* I needed to win."

Key Hand. The hand in a tournament that proves to be a turning point, for better or worse. "There is usually one *key hand* which, if you make it, will win the tournament for you. Unfortunately, it also goes the other way."

Kicker. The sidecard you hold in hold'em, the strength of which often determines who wins in a showdown. "I had a gorgeous hand, an A-Q with an ace showing on the board. But my beauty turned into a beast when Dana showed her A-K at the river to beat me with a better *kicker*."

Lay down your hand. Fold. "Sometimes you have to *lay down* your hand because it gets too expensive to play it."

Lead. You are the first one to enter the pot after the blind's forced bet. "T. J. *led out* with his A-K."

Level. In tournaments, the round that you are playing. A tournament level is defined by the size of the blinds. "At the $50-$100 *level*, I had only $800 in chips."

Limp (in). Enter the pot by calling, rather than raising, another player's bet. "You might decide to just *limp in* with a pair of jacks and see the flop cheaply."

Limper. A player who enters a pot for the minimum bet. "With two *limpers* in the pot, a pair of jacks should be your minimum raising hand."

Make a move. Try to bluff. "When Phil *made a move* at the pot, Huck called him down."

Maniac. A very aggressive player who sometimes plays hands his more sensible or conservative opponents would not consider. "*Maniacs* sometimes crash and burn earlier than they should in tournament play."

Mini-raise. In no-limit hold'em, you raise the minimum amount allowed, which is double the size of the big blind. "When Nguyen made a *mini-raise* from up front, I wondered whether he was trying to disguise a big hand, or just wanted to get into the pot cheaply."

Nuts. The best possible hand. "Nani won the pot when the A♠ fell on the river, giving her the *nut* flush."

Out(s). Cards that will improve your hand. If you hold a pair of sevens in hold'em and a seven is showing on the board, you have only one out to make quad sevens. "Looking at the board cards I figured that, with four sixes in the deck, I had only four *outs* to make my inside straight draw."

Overbet. You make a bet in no-limit hold'em that is far out of proportion to the size of the pot. "Some new players who don't understand how much to bet in no-limit hold'em often *overbet* the pot."

Payout. In a tournament, your payout is the amount of money that you will win if you finish among the top few finalists. "The *payout* for first place was 38 percent of the prize pool."

Play back. Responding to an opponent's bet by either raising or reraising. "If a tight opponent *plays back* at you, you know he probably holds the nuts."

Play fast. Aggressively betting and raising. "Many players *play fast* in the early rounds of rebuy tournaments to try to build their stacks."

Play with. Staying in the hand by betting, calling, raising, or reraising. "I wasn't sure exactly where he was at, so I decided to *play with* him on the turn."

Position (chip position). How your chip stack compares to the stacks of your opponents. "Going into the final two tables, Brad was in tenth *chip position*. Then he went on a rush and wound up winning the whole enchilada."

Position (table position). Where you are sitting in relation to the big blind. For example, if you are sitting one seat to the left of the big blind, you are in first position. "Eric was sitting in *middle position* with a K-J offsuit when Phil raised from a *front position*. Figuring Phil for a stronger hand than K-J, Eric wisely folded."

Position (have position on). You can act after someone else acts. For example, if you are sitting on the button in a hold'em game, you have position on your opponents. "I limped into the pot because Mad Max had *position on* me and I didn't want to get into too much trouble in case he decided to raise."

Positional raise. A raise that is based more on a player's table position than on the value of his cards. "Sure, I admit that it was just a *positional raise*, but it seemed right at the time."

Pot-logged. You have so many of your chips already invested in the pot that you are committed to going to the river with your hand. "When I called Dewey's reraise, I knew I'd be going all the way with my hand. What else could I do? By then, I was *pot-logged*."

Rag (or blank). A card that doesn't help you. "The next card was a 4♥, a total *blank*."

Ragged(y) flop. The cards in the flop are ones that do not appear to be able to help anyone's hand; i.e., there are no straight, flush, face cards, or pairs on board. "When the flop came *raggedy* with a 7-4-2, I knew Tight Ted didn't have any part of it."

Rail. The place from which spectators and losers watch the action. "When Brad made his flush at the river to beat my set of aces, I was forced to join the other losers on the *rail*."

Raise. Increase the bet. In limit hold'em, the amount that you can raise is prescribed, but in no-limit hold'em, you can raise any amount you want so long as you raise at least twice the size of the big blind. "When you get to the final table, you seldom just call. It's either *raise* or fold."

Read (your opponents). You can determine what your opponent is holding, or the significance of his betting strategy. "His play was so erratic, it was hard to *get a read* on him."

Read (the board). To understand how the board cards in hold'em relate to your hole cards. "You must be able to *read the board* well enough to tell whether you have the nuts or nothing at all, whether you have 16 outs or no outs."

Reraise. Raise the player who raised you. Sometimes there is more than one reraise during a hand. When the maximum number of reraises have been made, the pot has been capped. "Tom knew that Brad was trying to steal his blind by raising from the button, so he *reraised* him in defense."

Ring game. Not a tournament game; a cash game. "The side action *ring games* during tournaments can be lucrative."

Rise. A tournament term that refers to the increase of the blinds at the start of a new round or level of the tournament. "I knew the blinds would *rise* in three minutes, so I played a marginal hand while they were still at the lower amounts."

Rock. A very conservative player who always waits for premium cards before he plays a hand. "Smith was playing like a *rock*, so when she bet into me, I knew she had me beat."

Round. In tournaments, a round is a specified period of time during which the blinds remain the same. In a cash game, a round lasts for nine hands in a nine-handed game, ten hands in a ten-handed game. "In the $25-$50 *round*, I never had a playable hand," the tournament player lamented. "That's nothing," his buddy playing in the cash game said, "I just sat through three dry *rounds* where, from the small blind right through the button, I had to fold every hand."

Run over. Playing aggressively in an attempt to control the other players. "If they're not trying to stop you from being a bully, then keep *running over* them until they do."

Rush. A winning streak during which you might win four out of six hands, for example. "Robert is one lucky so-and-so. If he hadn't gone on that *rush* at the final table, I would've busted him in eight place."

Semi-bluff. You bet with a hand that probably isn't the best one at the moment, but which has a chance of improving. If everyone folds, your semi-bluff wins the pot for you; if someone calls, you still have a decent chance of winning. "Don's *semi-bluff* bet with only two overcards to the flop paid off when he caught an ace on the turn."

Slow down. Discontinue playing aggressively. "If Maniac Mike doesn't slow down in the late stage and start playing more conservatively, he's probably going to lose all those tournament chips he won with his early, aggressive play."

Smooth-call. You call rather than raise an opponent's bet. "Herb *smooth-called* me on the flop, but raised on the turn with his trip jacks."

Solid (player). A well-grounded player who thoroughly understands the game and plays it at a superior level. "You can depend on Knox to never get out of line. He's a *solid* player who always knows where he's at in a hand."

Splash around. Playing more loosely or more aggressively than you probably should. "Loose Louie *splashed around* too much with a big chip lead and went broke."

Stack. All of your chips. "I just don't have the temperament to play no-limit hold'em," Timid Tony said. "I can't bear the thought of possibly losing my whole *stack* at one time."

Stage. A tournament term that refers to a particular period during a tournament. Players usually think of a tournament as having an early stage, a middle stage, and a late stage, when only about three or four tables are left in action. "I caught three premium hands in the *middle stage* of the tournament, but I just couldn't hang on and bombed out in the *late stage* about three places out of the money."

Survival (mode). That time in a tournament when you are very short-stacked and begin playing very conservatively in order to survive for as long as you possibly can. "It was against my basic nature to shift into survival mode," Action Al said, "but I wanted to hang on long enough to give myself a chance to get lucky, as Tom McEvoy advised in his book, *Championship Tournament Poker*."

Take off a card. Calling a single bet in order to see one more card. "Tuna decided to *take off a card* to see if he could hit his inside-straight draw."

Tell. A playing habit or personal mannerism that a player consistently displays that enables his opponents to tell what he is holding or what he is likely to do during the play of a hand. "I noticed that every time Jake the Snake raised from early position with a weak hand, he sort of wobbled his chips into the pot, so I used his *tell* against him and reraised."

Throw away (a hand). Fold. "If Action Al raises from middle position, you might call with a K-Q, but if Solid Sam raises, you're probably better off to *throw your hand away*."

Throwing a party. Several loose or amateur players are making significant monetary contributions to the game. "You have to stay in the game when they're *throwing a party*."

Trap. You play deceptively in order to induce an unwise response from your opponent(s). "When Devious David limped into the pot from first position, I could small a *trap*. Turns out I was right: Loose Louie raised and David come over the top for all his chips."

Wake up with a hand. You are dealt a hand with winning potential. "It looked to me like Daugherty *woke up with a hand* in the small blind."

Where you're at. To know the value of your hand compared to your opponent's hand. "Hamid may have raised just to find out *where he was at*."

World's fair. A big hand. "Suppose the flop comes 8-8-4 in different suits: you know you're up against either nothing or *the world's fair*."

THE CHAMPIONSHIP SERIES
POWERFUL BOOKS YOU MUST HAVE

CHAMPIONSHIP HOLD'EM *by T. J. Cloutier & Tom McEvoy*. Hard-hitting hold'em the way it's played *today* in both limit cash games and tournaments. Get killer advice on how to win more money in rammin'-jammin' games, kill-pot, jackpot, shorthanded, and other types of cash games. You'll learn the thinking process before the flop, on the flop, on the turn, and at the river with specific suggestions for what to do when good or bad things happen plus 20 illustrated hands with play-by-play analyses. Specific advice for rocks in tight games, weaklings in loose games, experts in solid games, how hand values change in jackpot games, when you should fold, check, raise, reraise, check-raise, slowplay, bluff, and tournament strategies for small buy-in, big buy-in, rebuy, incremental add-on, satellite and big-field major tournaments. Wow! If you want to win at limit hold'em, you need this book! 392 pages, $29.95.

CHAMPIONSHIP NO-LIMIT & POT-LIMIT HOLD'EM *by T. J. Cloutier & Tom McEvoy*. This is the bible of winning pot-limit and no-limit hold'em tournaments. You'll get all the answers here —no holds barred—to your most important questions: How do you get inside your opponents' heads and learn how to beat them at their own game? How can you tell how much to bet, raise, and reraise in no-limit hold'em? When can you bluff? How do you set up your opponents in pot-limit hold'em so that you can win a monster pot? What are the best strategies for winning no-limit and pot-limit tournaments, satellites, and supersatellites? Rock-solid and inspired advice you can bank on from two of the most recognizable figures in poker. 304 pages, $29.95.

CHAMPIONSHIP OMAHA (Omaha High-Low, Pot-limit Omaha, Limit High Omaha) *by T. J. Cloutier & Tom McEvoy*. Clearly-written strategies and powerful advice from Cloutier and McEvoy who have won four World Series of Poker titles in Omaha tournaments. Powerful advice shows you how to win at low-limit and high-stakes games, how to play against loose and tight opponents, and the differing strategies for rebuy and freezeout tournaments. Learn the best starting hands, when slowplaying a big hand is dangerous, what danglers are and why winners don't play them, why pot-limit Omaha is the only poker game where you sometimes fold the nuts on the flop and are correct in doing so and overall, how can you win a lot of money at Omaha! 230 pages, photos, illustrations, $29.95.

CHAMPIONSHIP STUD (Seven-Card Stud, Stud 8/or Better and Razz) *by Dr. Max Stern, Linda Johnson, & Tom McEvoy*. The authors, who have earned millions of dollars in major tournaments and cash games, eight World Series of Poker bracelets and hundreds of other titles in competition against the best players in the world show you the winning strategies for medium-limit side games as well as poker tournaments and a general tournament strategy that is applicable to any form of poker. Includes give-and-take conversations between the authors to give you more than one point of view on how to play poker. 200 pages, hand pictorials, photos, $29.95.

THE CHAMPIONSHIP SERIES
POWERFUL BOOKS YOU MUST HAVE

HOW TO WIN NO-LIMIT HOLD'EM TOURNAMENTS by *Tom McEvoy & Don Vines*. Learn the basic concepts of tournament strategy, plus how to win big by playing small buy-in events, how to graduate to medium and big buy-in tournaments; how to adjust for short fields, huge fields, slow and fast-action events, plus how to win online no-limit tournaments; manage a tournament bankroll, and tips on table demeanor for televised tournaments. See actual hands played by finalists at WSOP and WPT championship tables with card pictures, analysis and useful lessons from the play. 376 pages, $29.95.

CHAMPIONSHIP WIN YOUR WAY INTO BIG MONEY HOLD'EM TOURNAMENTS by *Brad Dougherty & Tom McEvoy*. Every year, from 2002 to 2005, satellite players won their way into the $10,000 WSOP buy-in and emerged as millionaires or champions. You can too! You'll learn specific, proven strategies for winning almost any satellite. Covers the 10 ways to win a seat at the WSOP, how to win limit hold'em and no-limit hold'em satellites, one-table satellites, online satellites, plus the final table of super satellites. Includes a special chapter on no-limit hold'em satellites! 320 pages, $29.95.

CHAMPIONSHIP HOLD'EM TOURNAMENT HANDS by *T. J. Cloutier & Tom McEvoy*. An absolute must for hold'em tournament players, two legends show you how to become a winning tournament player at both limit and no-limit hold'em games. Get inside their heads as they think they way through the correct strategy at 57 limit and no-limit starting hands. Cloutier & McEvoy show you how to use skill and intuition to play strategic hands for maximum profit in real tournament scenarios and how 45 key hands were played by champions in turnaround situations at the WSOP. Gain tremendous insights into how tournament poker is played at the highest levels. 368 pages, $29.95.

CHAMPIONSHIP TOURNAMENT POKER by *Tom McEvoy*. Enthusiastically endorsed by more than 5 world champions, this is a must for every player's library. McEvoy lets you in on the secrets he has used to win millions of dollars in tournaments and the insights he has learned competing against the best players in the world. Packed solid with winning strategies for 11 games with extensive discussions of 7-card stud, limit hold'em, pot and no-limit hold'em, Omaha high-low, re-buy, half-half tournaments, satellites, strategies for each stage of tournaments. 416 pages, $29.95.

CHAMPIONSHIP TABLE (at the World Series of Poker) by *Dana Smith, Ralph Wheeler, & Tom McEvoy*. *Championship Table* celebrates three decades of poker greats who have competed to win poker's most coveted title. This book gives you the names and photographs of all the players who made the final table, pictures the last hand the champion played against the runner-up, how they played their cards, how much they won, plus fascinating interviews and conversations with the champions. This fascinating and invaluable resource book includes tons of vintage photographs. 208 pages, $19.95.

VIDEOS AND STRATEGIES BY MIKE CARO
THE MAD GENIUS OF POKER

CARO'S PRO POKER TELLS
$59.95 Two-Video VHS Set
$49.95 DVD
This video is a powerful scientific course on how to use your opponents' gestures, words and body language to read their hands and win all their money. These carefully guarded poker secrets, filmed with 63 poker notables, will bring your game to the next level. It reveals when opponents are bluffing, when they aren't, and why. Knowing what your opponent's gestures mean, and protecting them from knowing yours, gives you a huge winning edge. Says two-time World Champion Doyle Brunson: "Mike Caro's research will revolutionize poker!" Prepare to be astonished!

CARO'S POWER POKER SEMINAR
$39.95 VHS 62 Minutes
This powerful video shows you how to win big money using the little-known concepts of world champion players. This advice will be worth thousands of dollars to you every year, and even more if you're a big money player! After 15 years of refusing to allow his seminars to be filmed, Caro presents entertaining but serious coverage of his long-guarded secrets. The most profitable poker advice ever put on video.

CARO'S MAJOR POKER SEMINAR
$24.95 VHS 60 Minutes
Caro's poker advice in VHS format. Based on the inaugural class at Mike Caro University of Poker, Gaming and Life strategy. The material given on this tape is based on many fundamentals introduced in Caro's works and is prepared in such a way that reinforces concepts old and new. Caro's style is easy-going but intense with key concepts stressed and repeated. This tape will improve your play.

CARO'S PROFESSIONAL POKER REPORTS
Mike Caro, the foremost authority on poker strategy, psychology, and statistics, has put together three powerful insider poker reports. Each report is centered around a daily mission, with you, the reader, concentrating on adding one weapon per day to your arsenal.

These highly focused reports are designed to take you to a new level at the tables. Theoretical concepts and practical situations are mixed together for fast in-depth learning in these concise courses. *Caro's Professional Reports* are very popular among good players.

11 Days to 7-Stud Success. Bluffing, playing and defending pairs, different strategies for the different streets, analyzing situations—lots of information within. One advantage is gained each day. A quick and powerful method to 7-stud winnings. Essential. Signed, numbered. $19.95.
12 Days to Hold'Em Success. Positional thinking, playing and defending against mistakes, small pairs, flop situations, playing the river, are just some sample lessons. Guaranteed to make you a better player. Very popular. Signed, numbered. $19.95.
Professional 7-Stud Report. When to call, pass, and raise, playing starting hands, aggressive play, 4th and 5th street concepts, lots more. Tells how to read an opponent's starting hand, plus sophisticated advanced strategies. Important revision for serious players. Signed, numbered. $19.95.

POWERFUL POKER SIMULATIONS
A MUST FOR SERIOUS PLAYERS WITH A COMPUTER!
IBM compatibles CD ROM Win 95, 98, 2000, NT, ME, XP - Full Color Graphics

These incredible full color poker simulation programs are the absolute best method to improve your game. Computer opponents play like real players. All games let you set the limits and rake, have fully programmable players, adjustable lineup, stat tracking, and Hand Analyzer for starting hands. Mike Caro, the world's foremost poker theoretician says, "Amazing...a steal for under $500...get it, it's great." Includes free telephone support. "Smart Advisor" gives expert advice for every play in every game!

NEW!
Windows Versions
More Features!

1. TURBO TEXAS HOLD'EM FOR WINDOWS - $89.95 - Choose which players, how many, 2-10, you want to play, create loose/tight game, control check-raising, bluffing, position, sensitivity to pot odds, more! Also, instant replay, pop-up odds, Professional Advisor, keeps track of play statistics. Free bonus: Hold'em Hand Analyzer analyzes all 169 pocket hands in detail, their win rates under any conditions you set. Caro says this "hold'em software is the most powerful ever created." Great product!

2. TURBO SEVEN-CARD STUD FOR WINDOWS - $89.95 - Create any conditions of play; choose number of players (2-8), bet amounts, fixed or spread limit, bring-in method, tight/loose conditions, position, reaction to board, number of dead cards, stack deck to create special conditions, instant replay. Terrific stat reporting includes analysis of starting cards, 3-D bar charts, graphs. Play interactively, run high speed simulation to test strategies. Hand Analyzer analyzes starting hands in detail. Wow!

3. TURBO OMAHA HIGH-LOW SPLIT FOR WINDOWS - $89.95 -Specify any playing conditions; betting limits, number of raises, blind structures, button position, aggressiveness/passiveness of opponents, number of players (2-10), types of hands dealt, blinds, position, board reaction, specify flop, turn, river cards! Choose opponents, use provided point count or create your own. Statistical reporting, instant replay, pop-up odds, high speed simulation to test strategies, amazing Hand Analyzer, much more!

4. TURBO OMAHA HIGH FOR WINDOWS - $89.95 - Same features as above, but tailored for Omaha High-only. Caro says program is "an electrifying research tool...it can clearly be worth thousands of dollars to any serious player. A must for Omaha High players.

5. TURBO 7 STUD 8 OR BETTER - $89.95 - Brand new with all the features you expect from the Wilson Turbo products: the latest artificial intelligence, instant advice and exact odds, play versus 2-7 opponents, enhanced data charts that can be exported or printed, the ability to fold out of turn and immediately go to the next hand, ability to peek at opponents hand, optional warning mode that warns you if a play disagrees with the advisor, and automatic testing mode that can run up to 50 tests unattended. Challenge tough computer players who vary their styles for a truly great poker game.

6. TOURNAMENT TEXAS HOLD'EM - $59.95

Set-up for tournament practice and play, this realistic simulation pits you against celebrity look-alikes. Tons of options let you control tournament size with 10 to 300 entrants, select limits, ante, rake, blind structures, freezeouts, number of rebuys and competition level of opponents - average, tough, or toughest. Pop-up status report shows how you're doing vs. the competition. Save tournaments in progress to play again later. Additional feature allows you to quickly finish a folded hand and go on to the next.